Do You Know What Info Marketing Is?

This Book Will Show You How To Make A Profit

With A Digital Business !

Discover How To Earn Money With Your

Texts, Audio And Informative Videos!

(You Will Find 5 Manuscripts As Bonus Inside This Book!)

By : "Santiago Johnson Smith"

Disclaimer

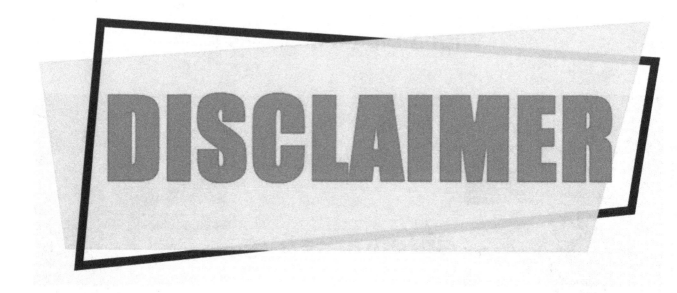

This e-book has been written to provide information only. Every effort has been made to make this ebook as complete and accurate as possible. However, there may be mistakes in typography or content.

Also, this e-book provides information only up to the publishing date. Therefore, this ebook should be used as a guide - not as the ultimate source. The purpose of this ebook is to educate. The author and the publisher does not warrant that the information contained in this e-book is fully complete and shall not be responsible for any errors or omissions.

The author and publisher shall have neither liability nor responsibility to any person or entity with respect to any loss or damage caused or alleged to be caused directly or indirectly by this e-book.

Table of Contents

INTRODUCTION

If you're a blogger, video marketer, internet marketer, or an information product creator you've no doubt struggled with the question of content. You can have the best ideas, but if you don't know how to use that idea to build quality content for a website, it probably won't be successful. When it comes to your website, every part is important. Sure you want the right font, color, design, etc. The most important part of your website, however, is your content. Without quality content, your website cannot survive. It is important to remember—Content is everything! When you first start your site, you give a great deal of time to picking out the perfect domain name.

There's a reason you select a good domain name. It's where your site lives. If your website is your domain, then think of content as the king of that domain. In other words...content rules! Many start-up businesses, and even established business owners who've decided it's time their business had a professional web presence, don't know where to start when it comes to planning their website. There are so many things to consider, and so many choices. Just getting the design and layout of the website can be intimidating. Then you have to determine what will be on the site. It can be mind-boggling. Sometimes, by the time you get to the content portion of the site, your brain is fried from trying to make the other decisions.

When you begin to think about the content, you're probably asking yourself, "What do I write about" or "Where do I start?" If so, you've come to the right place. You only have one chance to make that first impression. If you take your content seriously then your audience will too. You want your audience to visit your site over and over again. If you provide quality content for them time and time again, they will keep returning to your site. Getting started is the most important step.

If you know how to write, you are already 95% of the way there. You don't need to be an English major to understand any of the tips in this book either. It is written in plain English that everyone can understand. Writing for the internet requires different skills to those covered in most school writing lessons. If you've never been much of a writer, starting writing as an adult may seem difficult. The upside of that is that as an adult you have more experience, skills, and knowledge that you can share with your readers. This knowledge, skills and experience can be valuable to you and to others. Writing an article, series of articles, or blog posts can be an excellent way to share what you know and what you've experienced with your audience. While the writing you need for your site can be outsourced to professionals, it is very possible, and definitely more personal, for you to do it yourself. That's what the tips in this book can help you do. Professional content writers are exactly that, professional.

They take their jobs seriously. When a professional writer has been provided with instructions from a client, they read them carefully to get an understanding of what is required.

The problem with outsourcing to a professional is they don't know what you know or haven't experienced the things that you have. They don't know how you feel. In other words, they don't have your heart. They can write in the way you instruct them, but they can't write with your heart. They can give information, but they can't give a reader a sense of who you are. They can't share your personal experiences with the same passion you feel. Writing your own content can also be a very rewarding experience. It can help you make a personal connection with your readers.

It gives them a sense of who you are, because you will be sharing your knowledge, thoughts, and feelings in everything you write. Writing content that connects to your readers is what you want to do. If you've never written anything for a website before, don't worry. You're not alone. That's why you're reading this book.

The information here will help you create that quality content. For your convenience, the book is sectioned into the four main content areas: articles, blog posts, ebooks, and videos. Together, there are 70 great tips to give your website the "WOW" factor.

STEP IN WRITING PROCESS

Before you begin writing anything, it is important to understand the writing process. Writing is more than just putting words on paper. It takes thought and planning to produce quality content, and having quality content is more than important...it's imperative! Never has the phrase, "Anything worth doing is worth doing right," more important than when preparing content for your site. When you prepare to write an article, series of articles, blog posts, or even a script for a video for your site, ask yourself what you are going to write about and in what way are you going to talk about the topic.

Think about the final use of the article and tailor the article to suit its purpose. Think about it: is it promotion, informative article with an action involved from the reader, or is it purely for education purposes. There are many different ways to write and many approaches you can take. Look at all the ways you can approach the article, and select the best approach for your purpose. After you know your topic, brainstorm for ideas. This is simply writing down ideas and thoughts about the subject. Jot down all of the ideas you can come up.

They might seem silly at the time, but write them anyway. Jot down everything you can think of. You may find it helpful to keep some means of writing ideas with you at all times. It can be a note pad and pen, or an electronic device. Whichever it is, you'll be able to write down the ideas as they come to you. You don't have to use them all. You can decide that later. Just get yourcreative juices flowing and come up with anything relative to your topic. Think about who your audience will be. If you think about movies, they're rated for a reason. People don't begin a movie for a "G" rated audience in an "R" rated format.

Having an understanding of your audience will allow you to set a suitable tone and create content the audience finds value in. Will your readers be adult, children, or teenagers? Will they be male or female? Will they be educated or perhaps high school dropouts? Will there be a particular ethnic group more likely to read than others? All these things are important when you decide what you want to write and how you will go about writing it. You want to write to the audience in a way they can relate to what you've written and understand it. Research the topic you want to write about in detail to provide information that is not common knowledge. You may know a lot about the topic, in fact, it's better to have a good knowledge of what you're writing about, because you'll find it easier to write. There are, however, many resources you can use to find relevant content about a subject that you might not know about. You may find information about a topic you know well that you didn't know.

You may want to pull information from several different sources for one article. Just remember, when using these resources, it is important to rewrite the information in your own way. Do not copy information from other sites or you'll be guilty of copyright infringement. You should prepare an outline of your article, blog post, or ebook. Preparing an outline will help you to prepare quality content for your website. It keeps you focused and on track. You know that your content helps the websites web marketing, web ranking and content marketing efforts.

The outline will help you create a logical order and flow to what you write, and improve your chances of higher web rankings. Once the outline is complete, you're ready to begin writing. Follow the outline, and use the information you know or the information gathered from researching other resources to fill in the blanks. If you remember the "fill in the blank" tests from school, you'll know that this is an important part of the writing process. If you don't put the right words in the right blanks, you fail the test.

If you don't fill in the blank in the right way, your writing will fail. People will click on your site, begin reading, see it isn't quality content, and then click off. You've probably done that yourself many times. The internet makes it so easy it has become automatic to some people. Click on—read junk— click off.

It's as simple as that. Filling in the blanks properly, however, will cause people to click on to your site repeatedly. There are three major portions to any written material: Introduction, Body, and Conclusion. You should always start with a good introduction. Then you prepare the body, which is the meat of the material. Last, but certainly not least, is the conclusion. In the introduction you should tell the audience what you are going to tell them and what they can expect to learn. The body of the article will include the details about the topic and mention different points that will connect to the reader. These details should give the reader what you told them they were going to get. The conclusion is where you summarize and state any conclusions that the reader should have come to once they've read your material.

The conclusion is the last impression you will make on the readers, so you always want to go out in style. Let them leave feeling taking the time to read your material has been worth their while. Write your first draft without being over-critical. In your first draft, you're basically getting all your information down on paper in a fairly logical format. Then, you go back and revise the draft in a more critical manner. It often helps to read the article aloud.

As you do, make mental notes to fully pronounce every word. This will help you find grammar errors and inconstancy in the article. It will also help you keep a good, steady flow to your writing that isn't confusing. If you stumble over the words when you read it, so will your reader. Once you've completed reading the material and any errors have been corrected, you'll probably repeat the process again and again until the article is satisfactory to you. You may discover you need to:

• Rearrange paragraphs to make it flow better
• Reword awkward sentences
• Remove extra words, repetitive sentences, or even whole paragraphs

You need to realize that no one is perfect. Learning to write articles, blogs, or ebooks takes time, creativity, patience, and practice. You may feel you have something great and find out it wasn't so good after all.

Don't be discouraged if you have to change your draft several times before you get it right. Just remember, "If at first you don't succeed, try, try again." Once you have that article, blog, ebook, or video that you feel is "just right," it will be worth it. Not only will you feel great about yourself, you'll have quality content that is fit to reign. You'll be surprised. Once you have been through the process of writing your rough draft and editing the drafts a few times, you'll get used to all of these things. It will become automatic, unconscious competence writing and you'll wonder why you ever thought it would be so difficult to start with. If you follow the all of the above steps, before you know it you will be able to be a competent writer. Being a competent writer is the first step to creating that dynamic content you need for your website. Now, you know the writing process. It's time to take the information you know, follow the process, and begin creating content fit for a king. Below are 70 great tips to help you create that content you can be proud of. It will be the type of quality content that will keep your audience returning to your site for more.

WEB ARTICLE TIPS

1. Answer the questions: who, why, where, when, what and how. If you answer these questions, you are half way to writing a good article. You've no doubt read newspaper articles. Journalists always use this type of format. Practice reading news articles and identifying these six things. You'll see how journalists use them to create quality content for their newspaper. Then write your article in a similar fashion answering these questions.

2. Check grammar and spelling as you go and when you have finished the article. Nothing shows lack of professionalism more than an article full of misspelled words and poor grammar. Be sure to check for homonyms that spell check won't correct like: they're, their, there—to, two, too. You'll want to make sure you use the right form of each when you write. Sure, some people won't notice, but those who do won't take your information seriously if it's riddled with grammatical errors.

3. Give your article a good hook. This is the first impression the reader will have of your article. You could write the most fantastic, helpful article ever, have an average title, and it would never get read. This is one of the worst things that can happen to a great piece of writing. The trick is to have a good hook. Make it something that catches the reader' attention. Readers want to know that if they're going to spend time reading your work that it is going to be worth it. The best titles express exactly what the reader will take away from your article. A good hook in an article will reel your audience in again to see what you write next.

4. Prepare a good introduction. After your title, your introduction is your second impression you make on the reader and it is very important. If a reader sees a captivating title, clicks on it, and starts reading the first paragraph only to find it irrelevant or uninteresting, they're not going to waste another two seconds to read the second paragraph, let alone the rest of the article. Give them a reason to continue reading. Write something bold or controversial. Use a famous or entertaining relative quote. Tell them what they're going to learn from you, and then jump right in.

5. Organize your article well. Reading an internet article is much different than reading one in print. Generally, online, people tend to skim rather than actually read, regardless of what the content is. This makes organization and readability two key factors to consider when writing any online content. You can use subheadings, numbers, and bullets. Create bold subject headings or bulleted points throughout your article to guide your reader's eye and help speed-readers grasp the concepts quickly and more effectively.

6. Be yourself. This doesn't mean you have to write like you talk, but write in language that expresses your personality. Try not to use too much "technical jargon," and stay away from the Thesaurus. Big words do not equal a smarter, better article. Depending on your target audience, there may be times when it's important to use technical terms or bigger words. In general, however, you shouldn't have to use the dictionary to read an article online. If people have to do that, they not only will click off of your site, they won't care about the information you have to share. Just be yourself, and express who you are. Sure, you want your work to impress your readers. They can't be impressed, however, if they can't understand it. Just talk to them in a style you feel comfortable with, and they'll listen.

7. Use examples or tell a story. Articles with examples get the points across more effectively than those without them. Stories and examples help you engage the reader by putting the topic at hand in context and allowing them to see how the takeaways may be applied. Sometimes you read an article, and you think you understand the concepts, but you're not sure how to use them. If the writer tells a story or gives examples, then the reader won't have to wonder if they got it right. They'll see how those concepts can be used.

8. Do not tell your readers you're writing the article because you want their business. This is one of the worst things you can do. Simply share your information and show them how what you have to offer can apply directly to their business. If you do, they will begin to trust you and turn to you when they are ready, as you have already proved that you are a valuable resource.

9. Edit! Remember that "spell check" is important, but it doesn't get everything. Read and reread your article to make sure everything is correct. Make sure the flow is good, and it will make sense to the reader.

BLOG POST TIPS

10. Know the ins and outs of your blogging platform. This helps you be sure your posts look as good as they can. Take the time to master the visual editor (or raw HTML, if you prefer) so that you know how to format a post, insert an image and embed a video or podcast. If you're not comfortable with the more technical aspects of blogging, try to find someone who can be a resource for you to answer questions as they arise.

11. Establish categories and stay on topic. Whether your new blog post is a stand-alone post or part of a series you're writing, it should fit into your blog categories as well as your overall content strategy. Meaning that you want to stay on topic and have your posts fit into the categories you've established. When selecting your categories, ask yourself, if they make sense, and fit into the objectives of your business. Having clearly defined blog categories will help you continue generating meaningful content and topics for your blog.

12. Create a meta-description. Most search engines will use a maximum of 160 characters for your post description on their results pages. If you don't create a meta-description, which is a concise summary of your page's content, a search engine will often take the first 160 characters it finds on your page instead. This will not give the reader a full sense of what they'll get from reading your post. A planned description will give them an idea of why they should read your post, and make them want to read it.

13. Use an editorial calendar. Most bloggers find it helpful to use an editorial calendar for scheduling and organizing topics for posts. Some people use their calendars to track more elaborate details. This will help you produce consistently.

14. Create a good design for your site. In order for them to want to read your post, they have to stay on your site. The design is the first thing visitors see and it significantly influences bounce rate, page views, and conversions. Have a professional look, and they'll take you more seriously and be more apt to stay online to read the quality content you produce.

15. Identify five metrics to keep an eye on how your blogging is going such as: visitors, leads, subscribers, inbound links and social media shares. This will help you keep track of your viewers, and give you a greater sense of when you get it right, and when you don't.

16. Be sure to include your name, title, and a way readers can contact you. Readers are not only interested in the content in your blog post. They also want to know who wrote the post and their role at your organization.

Sometimes you'll come across a thoroughly researched and well-written post only to find an attribution of "admin." Even if the blog is only written by you and you're the administrator of the blog, let the readers know who you are.

17. Publish and promote your site. Publishing and promoting are important stages of creating a successful blog post. One thing you want to do during the publishing stage is to ensure that your post has some kind of call to action. Promoting a blog post can involve a fair amount of thought and strategy. Utilize blog commenting promotion and direct messaging partners in social media to see if they'll help spread the word. Take the time to build a good foundation before you expect to execute a successful blog promotion.

18. Try answering questions. One effective way to get content ideas for blogging comes from reviewing web analytics for the kinds of questions people type into search engines like Google or Bing that deliver visitors. If it is a popular question, giving people the answer they're looking for can help build your audience. You can also ask have your readers to write questions. When they do, you can take the answers for these questions and use them for future posts.

19. Make your work stand out. When you've been blogging for a while, chances are good that you'll see other bloggers writing on topics similar to yours. It doesn't mean that you have to stay away from the topic completely. Instead, you can take that opportunity to see what worked and didn't work in their post. Then, use that knowledge to write yours in a way that will help you to stand out in the topic area. You may find a few articles that have good "parts," but they fail to have a good "whole." If you use the information from the good parts of several articles to create your own article, yours will stand out. It will be good in its entirety.

20. Write user-centered/valuable content. One big mistake a blog post can make is missing the mark of its readers, forgetting who they are and their needs and interests. If the content is usercentered, and knowledgeable, it will be a greater value to the reader. You may begin with one target market in mind, and see that a different market is reading your articles. Change direction, and focus your blogs on the needs and interests of those users. Give someone what they want, and they'll come back to you again and again.

21. Make sure your content is understandable. Be sure to consider the reader's character, context and respect for the reader's reading level, articulate an old idea in a new way. You may want to give very technical information to an audience that isn't really educated. Break it down and present it in terms they can understand.

22. Make your content actionable. This means you should include a call to action, a place to comment, an invitation to share, links to related content, and a direct summary of what to do. If they can take part in what you blog, they'll feel like they're part of it. It will make them want to return.

23. Don't let the quantity of words dictate the quality of your post. Some blogs have set parameters for optimal length and put a value on whether a post is short or long. Instead of focusing on word count, a better use of your time and energy would be to focus on whether posts are optimized for mobile, use effective formatting, communicate in a clear manner and that outlining the points you want to cover. If you're restricted to shorter posts by the parameters set up in advance for your blog, you can link to longerform content you've developed around the topic. Remember quality content will always reign over quantity.

24. Determine what parts of yourself are you willing and able to share with your readers and share it. Readers like to get to know how about writers and often appreciate hearing a few personal details and insights from the person who has taken them on a journey through a post. Business blogs shouldn't be thought of as personal journal entries, however, you can tell your readers a little bit about how you operate.

25. Create a time and place where you can get into the zone for writing. While it's true that ideas for blog posts will come at all times, chances are good though that the actual writing of the post will happen in multiple drafts and revisions. Once you're in the zone, you can use those inspirations that came to you when you're driving in your car, sitting at your desk, or even in the middle of the night, and go with them.

26. Begin with the ending in mind. Think of an inverted pyramid when you write. Get to the point in the first paragraph. Let them know what they're going to take away from your post, and then expand upon it.

27. Write short sentences. Sentences need to be concise. Use only the words you need to get the essential information across. Long "wordy" sentences can make a post difficult to read, especially when you're scanning.

28. Write only one idea per paragraph. Web pages need to be concise and to-the-point. As with articles, most people usually scan web posts, so having short, meaty paragraphs is better than long rambling ones.

29. Write with action words. Tell your readers what to do. Avoid the passive voice. By using action words, it will help you keep the flow of your pages moving and make it more exciting for your reader. Give them the actions they need to take to do something, and then tell them what they'll achieve by doing it.

30. Include internal sub-headings. When you use sub-headings, you make the text easier to scan. Your readers will move to the section of the document that is most useful for them, and internal cues make it easier for them to do this.

31. Make your links part of the copy. Links will also help your readers scan pages. They stand out from normal text, and provide clues as to what the page is about.

32. Put your readers at ease. You are not writing for a medical journal or literary society. You're writing to your peers on the Internet. Write in a simple style. If you introduce new terms, define them for your readers. Make them feel comfortable reading your material. Everyone enjoys a good read. Make your readers feel comfortable when they read, and they'll feel your post is a good read.

33. Don't be afraid to share your trade secrets. The more you tell, the more the demand you will create for your goods and services. The more information you give, the more likely people will understand that you really are an authority on the subject that you are speaking about. You've probably heard the phrase, "Give and it shall be given unto you." Give readers the information they want, and they'll give you their business.

34. If you are a business, emphasize the benefits of your product or service. Benefits are what sell, not features. The benefits may be that people can get these items in one place without shopping around, that they can save time and money, etc. You should mention the benefits that you offer to your potential customer often. Everyone wants to know, "What will I get from this?" Emphasize that, because that's what's important to them, and they will want your product or service, because it's a means to get that benefit. You already know what your customers are curious about and what they need to make their lives easier. Use that knowledge to create your website content articles to give them new information and help them find what they are looking for.

35. Give your readers resource information. Let your readers know the addresses of websites where they can get more information on the subject that you are talking about. These can be your own websites or they can be other resources. Don't worry about losing customers. Good outgoing links from your website are also helpful to your site's page ranking and positioning in search engines.

36. Get a second opinion. Getting another opinion isn't only necessary when it's a medical issue. Get another opinion on your article. Show it to your friends and colleagues. Don't worry if they criticize you. It is better that your friends find the mistakes than your readers. A good editor is a writer's best friend.

37. Be straight forward. Talk to your reader. Write in a style that sounds just like you are chatting directly with them. This will engage their interest. Imagine you are sitting over a cup of coffee with them and write. That way you should avoid being too longwinded.

38. Write what you know. Knowledge is power. Choose subjects you are familiar with. If you do, writing will be less of a chore when you feel comfortable with the subject. If you know your topic well and you're passionate about what you're writing, that passion will show through. It will help the reader feel it when they read.

39. Enjoy yourself when you write. You've probably tried to read a book and failed. It's almost impossible to read books or articles we don't enjoy, so it figures that writing books and articles becomes more difficult when we don't enjoy what we are writing about. Since posts are written regularly, they can sometime feel like a chore. Even as children we learn to hate chores. Writing about things you enjoy will make it more enjoyable to write. This way, you'll be writing because you WANT to...not because you feel you HAVE to.

40. Be consistent with your postings. This is extremely important to creating quality content for any platform. Many times, writers start projects with enthusiasm and energy. If they don't see results right away, they stop. Readers want some expectation of when they will see a new post from you, so be consistent. You don't have to post every day, but if you decide to write once a week, don't skip. Let the reader know when they can expect the next post from you. You can add things like, "Come back next Thursday for more great tips on how to…" If they like what they read this time, they'll write it down to visit your site again on that day for more information.

41. Re-purpose your content. You can use a good video you made, and create a post from it, get the video transcribed, or create a slideshow version, audio/podcast version, etc. You can also take your good postings and do short videos. Not everyone likes to read, and some would rather read than watch videos. This way, you're getting your content out there in many formats, so you can reach a wider audience.

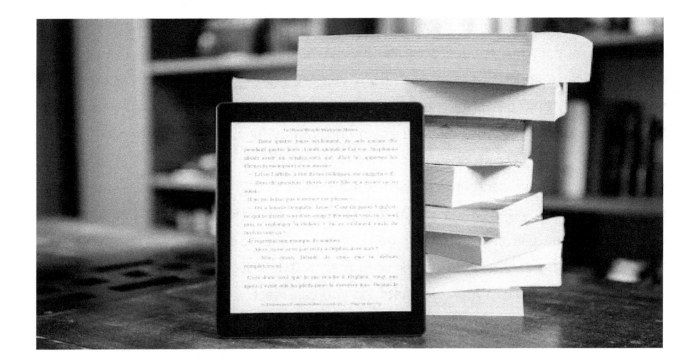

42. Don't let anyone tell you how hard it will be or that you can't write. This will discourage you and keep you from doing something you really want to do. If you're preparing to write your first ebook, this is the most important tip. Some of the most famous writers couldn't put a period or comma in the right place. It is more important to get those words down where they can become more real to you. This is the biggest step you can take. Editing can come later.

43. Break it down into manageable tasks. Remember, a journey of a thousand miles begins with the first step. The hardest part of writing is the title, first sentence and a potential ending line. Breaking it down makes each task seem smaller and more manageable. When you look at the whole project, it seems like an impossible task, but if you can get the project started, even if not perfectly, at least you have begun to get the words down on paper.

44. Figure out a good working title. Don't just pick one out of thin air and say, "This is the name of my book." Write down a few different titles and eventually you'll find that one that starts to grow on you. Titles help you to focus writing on your topic. They guide you in anticipating and answering your readers' questions. Don't pick a title, and then write about something that doesn't go with it. The title should let the reader know what the ebook is about.

45. Have a good thesis statement. Your thesis is a sentence or two stating exactly what problem you are addressing and how your book will solve that problem. Your thesis will keep you focused while you write. Each chapter comes from your thesis statement. Once you've got your thesis statement fine-tuned, you'll have your foundation. You build on that foundation and build your book chapter by chapter.

46. Be sure there is good reason to write your book, a niche for it to fill in society. The internet is a great place for niche content, because your potential audience is global, not local. This will increase your odds of connecting with people who want what you have to offer. Determine if your book will:

• Present useful information and is that information currently relevant
• Positively affect the lives of your readers
• Be dynamic and will it keep the reader's attention
• Answer questions that are meaningful and significant.

47. Give up on writing the book that will be cherished by all. It won't happen. You will be writing to your targeted audience, and they should dictate many elements of your book. They will help determine thing such as: style, tone, diction, and even length. The more you narrow down your target audience, the greater chance your ebook will have of success.

Determine the following:

- Expected age range of your readers
- Typical gender
- Readers main interests
- Socio-economic group they're from

48. Write down your publishing goals before you write. The more you know up front, the easier the actual writing will be. Do you want to sell it as a product on your website, or do you want to offer it as a free gift? The more you know about how you plan to publish it, the more you can write toward that goal.

49. Use fairly consistent chapter format. Perhaps you plan to use an introduction to your chapter topic, and then divide it into four subhead topics. You may plan to divide it into five parts, each one beginning with a relevant story or experience. Whatever format you choose, make sure to be consistent with it throughout your book.

50. Keep your writing engaging. Usually, anecdotes, testimonials, little stories, photos, graphs, advice, and tips will keep the reader reading the pages. You can also use sidebars which are useful for quick, accessible information. This will help break up the density of the page.

51. The most important tip when writing anything is: Make backups of all work. There is nothing worse than having your book almost finished only to lose it.

52. Have anyone you let read it initial and date a hard copy. In the internet world, plagiarism and copyright infringement is a big problem. If you have someone do this, it provides some confidence that if it happens you will have some record of the fact that you wrote it, and when you wrote it.

VIDEO TIPS

53. Remember that success is relative. For you, success might be something completely different from someone else. If you start judging your own level of success by somebody else's standards, you're setting yourself up for failure. Have your own success goals. Set your own heights, and then begin to climb.

54. Purchase good cameras. You may be surprised at the number of videos on sites or YouTube that aren't even watchable. Buying good cameras should go without saying, but some people don't realize how important it is. You'll probably experiment with a variety of devices, and always be looking at newer, better solutions for your efforts. Remember when you make your camera choice: People will complain about bad video, but people never complain about a video looking too good.

55. High resolution will bring higher quality. If you can record your videos in high definition, do it. High definition resolution is 1920 × 1080 pixels is what YouTube will host for you. It is quite affordable. You can record in this size without spending much more than a few hundred dollars. The results will speak for themselves.

56. Purchase a good microphone. You don't need to go all-out when it comes to basic audio equipment. You won't need much more than a USB port to find a mic that is worth using. You want one that sounds clear without being "fuzzy," and one that doesn't make noises every time you move. You may come across times when getting good audio is impossible, but that should be the exception, not the rule.

57. Have good lighting. This is especially true if you are doing a product review or demonstration. People need to see what it is you are showing them. You probably won't need stage lighting, but using sufficient light to show the details within your scene is crucial to producing a good video.

58. Create a good scene. Don't just randomly hit the record button. Think before you begin. Know what you're going to say, and take note of your surroundings. It's hard to take someone seriously if behind them is a sink full of dirty dishes or junk scattered all over their dresser or desk. It's distracting to viewers. You may be making amateur content for the Web but it doesn't mean you have to look unprofessional.

59. Remember you only have about 15 second to get someone's attention. If you don't have much of a personality on camera, you might as well not record. You need to let the real you shine through. If you're not very energetic, maybe you should consider sticking to the written form of communication. Just because you can record video doesn't mean you should. If a viewer clicks on your video and it doesn't catch their attention in the first 15 second, they just click out.

60. Always practice. Watching other people isn't going to make you better. Practice your video content, and try recording some samples and upload them as private videos. You can send the links to your friends and family, and ask them for feedback. It will probably take several takes to get it right. Watch every one of your takes, and select the one you like most.

61. Don't make something more complex than it needs to be. If your effort is overwhelming you, it's not going to be fun. If it's not fun, then you're not likely to stick with it for long. This rule also applies to your viewer. If what you're presenting is overwhelming them, they won't watch it.

62. Stay on topic when you record. People tend to ramble. This is particularly true when they're nervous. It is also true if they're interested in a topic. If you ramble, try to keep it relevant to the reason you're recording your video. You may need to refer to notes, when you first start recording. If you do, that's fine. Just stay on topic. No one wants to hear about your Great Aunt Sally's hernia surgery in the middle of your "How to" presentation just because it pops into your head. If you're not doing the presentation on "How to overcome surgical procedures," it wouldn't be relative.

63. Keep an energetic voice. You don't want to put people to sleep with your videos. If you have no energy in your voice, you're not going to keep people listening for long. Keep your video lively and energetic, and people are more apt to stick through to the end. You probably remember a teacher or college professor that spoke in a monotone voice that caused you to nod off a few times. You couldn't click out, because you had to be there. Online, however, they can click out, and they will.

64. Try using humor. Comedy has worked for generations. Why? Because funny is good, especially when it's unexpected. Funny is, however, is relative, so don't push it. Lightheartedness in videos breaks down barriers. A controlled amount of silliness can be fun, and entertaining. I'm not saying you should be a comedian, just add a bit of humor to make it stand out and keep your viewer attentive.

65. Give people something to look forward to. If you have a regular schedule for something to happen, like a live giveaway on Saturday, people will be in the live chat waiting anxiously for that giveaway. It's something they can look forward to each week. Giveaways might not be your thing, that's OK. Whatever you do, however, you need to have a routine people can put on their calendar and make a habit out of.

66. Give your viewers a reason to send your video links to their friends. There are a lot of people who don't use YouTube's search tool, but they do rely on the opinions of others. If someone comes across your video and finds it interesting, helpful, or funny, your chances of having them send it to someone they know increases. This is also true if you are creating useful content. These things help others want to "Favorite" your videos, embed them in their blogs or social profiles, or share your creations with their friends via instant messages or email. You can even say, "If you like this video and know someone who will enjoy it, be sure to send them the link." It will make them think, "Oh, I bet Bob would like this," and they'll pass it on.

67. Don't let them go without knowing where you are. Don't rely on descriptions and tags for everything. Everything you want to convey must be within the video itself. Tell the viewer know who you are. Chances are, if they're watching the video, they would rather watch than read. If you don't tell them, they may never know.

68. Ask your audience feedback. You're already presenting a callto-action in every video. Ask your viewers for feedback. It may not always be positive, so be prepared for both positive and negative remarks. Take pride in the positive ones, and learn from the negative ones. Use these comments to create your future videos with even more quality content.

69. Treat each one of your videos as though it were the only video of yours they will ever watch. Each video should stand alone. Often, people want to do a series of videos. That's great, however, someone may only catch your video on number three. It should be complete, from beginning to end. Those who watch numbers one and two will know what three is about, but this new viewer won't. Give a brief review of one and two before you go on to three. This way, that video will be complete, and they'll know they want to watch one and two so they can understand the whole process and be eager for number 4. You'll know every viewer will have heard things like your signature sign-on/off, but use them each time to make each video complete within itself.

70. Use annotations and tags. You can use the annotation feature to place call outs or hyperlinks to any other page on YouTube. They'll display over your videos on YouTube and in all embeds. That's all the more reason to use the "note" annotation, which allows for the insertion of YouTube URLs. Tags will help people be more likely to find your videos through searches. Tags are nothing more than keywords, linking people to videos which also contain the same tags. Not only will this help you attain more views from YouTube searches, it'll also help classify your own videos on YouTube.

CONCLUSION

We are living in the age of technology. If you don't have a website for your business, you need to get one. You'll want that site to have quality content for your articles, blogs, etc. Quality content includes other things as well. You'll probably need to write a brief introduction of your business and tell what it has to offer. You may want a biography section that tells about yourself.

You may want a company mission statement. Each of these sections of your website should be written with care, and give your audience quality information about you or your business.

If you choose to include these portions on your site, be sure to use objective language to build credibility, rather than exaggerated claims or overly promotional words like "great", "tremendous" etc. Online readers are skeptical. Credibility is a major factor in retaining reader interest on the Web. One way to help build credibility is to use hyperlinks to the sources of your information or to related information. Remember when you write that in an average workday, people suffer from information overload. They already have a lot of emails in their inbox to deal with, and several documents to read. They don't want to spend time and effort reading content that they may not find useful.

They want to read content that is a benefit to them. Choosing the right keywords and phrases for your website is an important part of the process of search engine optimization. It helps make your site more visible to search engines and searchers alike. Try to have one to three related keyword phrases that are site-specific.

To use keywords effectively:

• Be creative, but be choosy.
• Try not to target keyword phrases that are too competitive.
• If there are unusual words associated with your content that you think people might search for, or misspellings, include them sparingly.

Keywords written within your material will help increase traffic. Increasing your website traffic may be time-consuming, but search engine optimization today is primarily focused around providing a great experience for the visitors to your website. That's why quality content is SO important.

Always think before you publish or post things on your site. As obvious as this may seem, it is not always followed. A lot of people trust the opinions and information they read online. Don't pretend to be expert on subjects or give out bad advice.

Some people will take the information as gospel. Junk information on your site can never be considered quality content. It seems like practically everyone has a website nowadays. To stand out in the crowd and rise above other sites, you want to use helpful suggestions regarding content, facts—not fiction, and quality writing. You should never consider your website "complete."

If you want it to survive in the online world, you need to treat your site like a "living" thing that will change over time. It's something that will grow as you grow in knowledge and experience. It will grow as your business grows. In its infancy, you will find many things you want to change. Over time, you will find what works on your site and what doesn't. You will grow your site into a mature site with quality content and a large audience that proves it.

This book wasn't intended to turn you into a literary genius. You may not win a literary prize, but if you follow the steps that in this book, you will be able to produce quality content for your website that could become the key to success in your Internet endeavors. In other words, your content will be king!

EARN MONEY WITH DIGITAL PRODUCTS

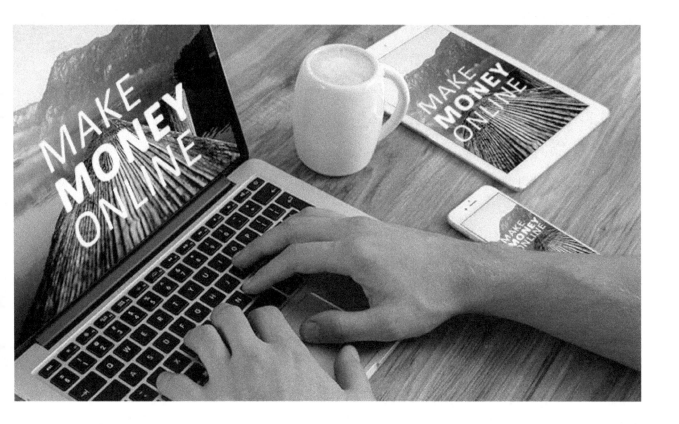

**This Book Will Show You How To Sell Your Digital Products
Or The Ones Own By Third-Party.**

<u>This Is The First Bonus Book</u> !

BY : "Santiago Johnson Smith"

Legal Notice

While all attempts have been made to verify information provided in this publication, neither the Author nor the Publisher assume any responsibility for errors, omissions, or contrary interpretation of the subject matter herein.

This publication is not intended for use as a source of legal or accounting advice. The Publisher wants to stress that the information contained herein may be subject to varying state and/or local laws or regulations. All users are advised to retain competent counsel to determine what state and/or local laws or regulations may apply to the user's particular business.

The Purchaser or Reader of this publication assumes responsibility for the use of these materials and information. Adherence to all applicable laws and regulations, federal, state, and local, governing professional licensing, business practices, advertising, and all other aspects of doing business in the United States or any other jurisdiction is the sole responsibility of the Purchaser or Reader.

The Author and Publisher assume no responsibility or liability whatsoever on the behalf of any Purchaser or Reader of these materials. Any perceived slights of specific people or organizations are unintentional.

Table Of Contents - 1°Bonus - [Earn Money With Digital Products]

The Sales Funnel Formula

Earnings Per Click

How To Win The Joint Venture

Joint Venture Commission Rates

How To Find Joint Venture Partners

How to Pull Off a Successful Joint Venture Invitation

Joint Venture Page For Affiliates

Launch Time

3-Step Launch Plan

Product Launch Techniques

Launch Overview

The internet has revolutionized small businesses and taken them to the next level. Nowadays, it is possible for anyone with an internet connection to create profit online by marketing products to eager, targeted buyers.

The best part is that you don't need a big wad of cash to get started – the internet marketing game is low cost, with sky-rocketing profits! While affiliate marketing is a popular option for people who just want a little extra side income, the big bucks come from product launches.

This will be the focus of this book – helping you create and refine your product launch, so that it becomes an irresistible offer that can't be refused.

We'll guide you through market research and how to create a digital product for your launch. You will also learn how to write and produce a sales letter that will grip your audience and coax them into purchasing your product. You will also discover the tactics behind successful promotional and marketing materials.

Later on, you'll learn the sales funnel secrets to boost your earnings per click. You'll also find out how to make your Joint Ventures and Partnerships more profitable, so that you're always on top.

We'll also tell you how to optimize your product launch so that you get the most out of it – from your pre-launch marketing strategies to even timing your launch. And in the final chapter, you'll learn how to boost your sales and make your product launch a sure-fire hit using specific, tried-and-tested techniques.

Now, before we go into all that, let's cover the basics of any product launch.

Products

Product launches are not a new innovation – they've been going on for ages. Launching your product online is something which you can successfully do as long as your product and marketing efforts are in sync. In internet marketing, when we talk about product launches, 99% of the time, we mean digital products. Think products like e-books, video tutorials, online courses, software and online membership sites – anything that is downloadable or accessible via a computer browser.

You don't even need to create the product from scratch if you don't want to – you can purchase Private Label Rights (PLR) material online. These are products which you can purchase and, in most cases, resell and claim as your own. We'll discuss these further in the following chapters.

Why You Should Create A Product Launch

New Product Launch

There are many other business ventures which you could take on in this day and age, so what makes product launches so great?

Fast Results & Flexibility

Firstly, you can get fast results and work flexibly. This is a point that doesn't need much explanation – we all know that product launches can bring in crazy profits, within just a few minutes!

Because your product is launched on the internet where there are millions of people online at any given time who are only a few clicks away from purchasing your product, it is insanely easy for your earnings to snowball within the first couple of hours of your launch.

On top of this, product launches give you so much flexibility – you can craft and prepare your launch from home, a café, while you're at your day job or even while on holiday!

With all the tools you need for your launch being accessible via the internet, you don't need to ever worry about being caught off guard. You can launch your product with just your laptop and a stable internet connection.

Not only that, you also have flexibility in terms of configuring your launch – with websites like JVZoo, ClickBank and Warriror+ Plus, you have so many options and customizations which you can use to tailor your product launch effectively.

Low-cost

Another benefit of launching your product online is it is a lot cheaper than launching physical products like t-shirts and books. If you think about it, creating and launching a digital product costs next to nothing.

When it comes to creating your digital product, sometimes all you need is Microsoft Word or an equivalent – tools which any basic laptop or desktop readily has. And by creating just one digital product, say a PDF format e-book, you can sell it to thousands of customers – it's like a one size fits all kind of situation so you have no need to reproduce the item again and again.

As for launching your product, a lot of websites will allow you to launch and promote your product for free in exchange for a small commission fee on each purchase. What this means is that you have no risk of losing any money – because even if your product doesn't make a single sale (which is a real rarity in this business), you won't be charged or penalized in any way.

Immediacy & Ease Of Purchase

Another awesome thing about product launches is that products can be delivered to your customers with just a few clicks of a mouse or If you have an autoresponder set up, your digital product can be forwarded to your customers instantly! This is a huge deal when compared to physical products, which sometimes take weeks to ship and tend to incur high shipping costs.

Your customers will receive their products in an e-mail or download within seconds of them completing their purchase – which is also something that can be optimized for ease of use.

When you launch your product, say on JVzoo or ClickBank or Warrior+ Plus, you will be able to customize the payment process to make it extremely easy for your customers. With the help of buy buttons, PayPal and autoresponders, customers can purchase your product without any hassle.

Build Your List

Your e-mail list is one of the most important aspects when it comes to your online marketing success. And the best way to grow your list is by launching products online. When someone purchases your product, you will also get a hold of their e-mail address, which you can add to your mailing list.

Through a list, you get to identify qualified leads, build relationships and most importantly, have a market that you can tap into whenever you want. Product launches help you add fresh leads to your list.

These e-mail addresses are valuable because for all of your oncoming products, you will have people who you can market to immediately by sending them a simple e-mail. A list gives you on-demand traffic whenever and wherever you want traffic to go. And it's not only helpful for just your own products - this list can come in handy if you are also an active affiliate marketer or engage in ad swapping.

Sell all your other products and services

Creating a product launch also lets you sell your other products and services. Usually, a buying frenzy ensues when you send your prospects through your sales funnel, after carefully selecting your upsells and downsells.

With upsells and downsells, you can entice your prospects to purchase some of your other products – this means that from the launch of a single product, you are able to also market one, two or even three other products to your prospect. That means you have the opportunity to further increase your profits.

Build Your Credibility and Affiliate Network

With the high quality content that you create and subsequently launch, you get to increase your credibility. You can solidify your status in your niche as a reliable expert.

On top of this, product launches are great ways to generate new partnerships and business relationships. A successful product launch will not only get the big players in the market interested in what you have to do and say, but there's also the high chance that you will be able to greatly expand your affiliate network. It's one of the many reasons why product launches are too lucrative an opportunity to say 'No' to.

How to Launch Your Product

1. Create or Find Your Product

2. Plan and Create a Sales Funnel

3. Create a Sales Letter & Sales Page

4. Find affiliates to promote your launch

5. Send Out Promotional E-mails

In a nutshell, there are five key steps that are involved in launching a product.

Firstly, you need to create your product. This includes conducting your niche and market research before you start actually creating a product. As mentioned earlier, you can also look for re-sellable PLR products.

PLR products listed on online marketplaces will usually come with a list of rights. So before you make a purchase, just make sure that the product you are purchasing also gives you the rights to reselling.

Once you have your product, you need to plan and create your sales funnel. A sales funnel is a great way to get your prospects to purchase your other offers. For most internet marketers and vendors, the sales funnel is where they get the bulk of their profit. Once you've set up your sales funnel, the traffic from your launch will immediately flow into it, which will help you generate even more sales.

For Step 3, you need to create your sales letter and sales page. The content of your sales letter is very important in getting people to purchase your product. Once you've produced your sales letter, be sure to also set up your sales page and ensure that all the links are working fine.

You can then move on to finding affiliates. These are the people who will help to promote your product in exchange for commission. This is the way to generate crazy traffic during your launch – if you only promote to your own followers and leads, you will not get the best results. Using affiliates helps your launch reach a wider audience and is therefore vital to your launch success.

Once that's done, you need to schedule and send out promotional emails to your list. There is an art to this, so that your e-mails get opened and aren't just brushed aside or worse – labeled as spam or junk. Be very particular when creating these e-mails, as they can really help your product sell well.

Where to Launch Your Product

Now that you know the basics of how to launch a product, let's take a quick look at where you can launch your product. While you can choose to launch your product independently, many online businesses choose to launch their product through an online marketplace. This is because it's really easy to customize your launch, plus with so many affiliates concentrated on these sites, it's a great opportunity to create hype for your product. There are 3 main platforms which internet marketers flock to, namely ClickBank, JVZoo and Warrior+ Plus.

One of the best things about ClickBank is the marketplace. Having your product listed in the marketplace is a great way to keep the buzz going, especially if you get you product to rank highly. The more interested people are in your product, the higher ranked your product will be – this means even more visibility and opportunities.

ClickBank is also a great place for you to launch your product if you aren't too picky about your affiliates. If your product is listed in the marketplace, ClickBank allows anyone on its site to become an affiliate by simply generating a unique affiliate link. If you are a little more particular about who promotes your product as an affiliate, you might want to go with JVZoo. JVZoo allows you to have complete control over who becomes an affiliate for your product, as you need to manually prove interested affiliates. With JVZoo, you can have interested parties message you first before you approve them as affiliates.

Another great thing about JVZoo is, comparable to ClickBank, it is a lot easier to use and they can host your product and sales page for you. This sort of gives you a one-stop checkpoint when you want to launch your product. Also, there is no upfront fee for launching your product on JVZoo. And, if you choose to, your product can be eligible for JVZoo's Pick Of The Day, which basically translates into even more visibility for your product.

As for our third option Warrior+ Plus, this is the best place to go to really exponentially grow your affiliate network – it has loads more affiliates to promote your product. And, like JVZoo, you also have the chance of your product being selected as pick of the day, which will surely attract even more affiliates. While Warrior+ Plus is a little older and not as user-friendly as ClickBank or JVZoo, in truth, the greatest value in launching your product on Warrior+ Plus is it is very saturated with people from the Internet Marketing niche. So if you are in that niche, Warrior+ Plus is the way to go - especially if you want to start getting your name out there.

Irresistible Offer Creation Secrets

In this chapter we're going to talk about all the work that goes into creating a best-selling offer. Your product launch is only going to be as good as your product, after all.

Finding And Knowing Your Niche

Before you start creating your product or offer, what you need to do is conduct thorough research. Researching your niche and analyzing the current trends in the market will help you create a must-have product which is in demand.

Your niche, and the findings from your research, will determine almost every aspect of not just your product but also your launch campaign.

As a general rule of thumb, the online marketing arena is primarily dominated by these three umbrella niches :

1)   The Health and Fitness niche

2)   The Online Business and Internet Marketing niche

3)   The Personal Development niche

These three niches are wide and generic, with more specific sub-niches within them and when it comes to defining your niche, you need to be as specific as possible. Having a focused target will make your product easier to market, compared to coming up with a product which is too general. A product that isn't focused can end up being a mix of too many things.

For example, let's say you have a product for the Internet Marketing niche. The Internet Marketing niche has so many different aspects to it. You could talk about Affiliate Marketing, which has its own following or you could be talking about How To Perform SEO for Your Website. Each of these titles would have their own following and the clearer you can establish your product, the easier it will be for interested prospects to find your product later on.

You can search for established sub-niches by simply pulling up a search on Google. Type in your keyword or umbrella niche and see what comes up in the search results. Also, look closely at the "Searches related to" section at the bottom of your Google Search results page. It's a goldmine of sub-niches which you can tap into. And remember – the more specific, the better.

Monitoring Activity

Once you've discerned your chosen niche or sub-niche, you need to check if it's got an active following. You can ascertain how active a niche is by monitoring their online activity. You want to see how many people are talking about the niche and you also want to find out if they are also active buyers. This is especially important, because you don't want to go into a niche that has a huge following but won't pay for products.

When it comes to finding out how active a niche is and what their spending habits are like, doing a quick and easy Facebook search is one of the easiest methods.

What you need to do is look for groups on Facebook which are related to your chosen niche. You only need to use the Facebook search bar on the top of the page.

For example, try typing in 'affiliates' or 'affiliate networks'. Then, check through the results and if you can find many groups that have hundreds of members, that's good. If most of the groups have got thousands of members, then that's an even better sign.

Try to find open groups that you can join. Look at their newsfeed. When was the last post? How many new posts do they get on average? And most importantly, do they share and sell products? Are people talking about the latest products and items that cater to the niche? Do they talk about their purchases? If the answer is 'yes' to all of this then congratulations – you've found yourself a niche market that is definitely worth looking into.

Conducting Product Research

Once you've nailed down your niche (which you now know for a fact has a big following), it's time for you to look into how you can effectively sell to that market. The best way to do this is by monitoring the products sold within that niche.

Do a scroll through on the Facebook pages again and look for the most talked about products. Try going one step further and read up on the common questions, dilemmas and problems that these active users go through. This will help you create a hot-selling product because the best products are the ones which offer timely solutions to common problems. It's a supply and demand scenario – you need to know what your target market is looking for, so that you can create a product which caters to those wants and needs.

On top of this, you can also go ahead and find products that are related to your niche by doing a search on Warrior+ Plus, ClickBank, or JVZoo. These online marketplaces have an eclectic collection of products that you can search through. If there's a niche for it, you'll definitely be able to find related products on these three websites.

As you're starting your product research, you want to focus on the products which are top sellers. You can usually find them in the main pages of all the marketplaces. Look for items that are of a high rank, especially if they've been voted as Pick of The Day or similar.

And the research doesn't just stop there. Why limit yourself to just the product listings on these marketplaces when you can dive in even deeper?

First of all, you can go ahead and look at the sales pages of these best-selling products. This will help you understand a little more about the tone, look and feel which is considered attractive in your chosen niche and you can craft your product to match that.

To learn more about the type of content that appeals to your audience, get your hands on free content related to your niche. You can even consider going the extra mile by purchasing a product, so that you can conduct thorough research. Do this with as many products as you can for your niche so that you'll learn what sort of information sells well in your chosen niche. This research will help you in so many ways – not just when it comes to creating your product. All this will come in handy when it is time to design your sales letter and create eye-catching sales copy.

If you look closely, you will be able to discern a pattern – some titles sell and some don't. What you want to do is find inspiration for your product, so that your finished product profitable and worth the time and effort that you put into it.

Digital Products

Once you've done your research, you can move on to creating your digital product. But before you start creating content, you should consider the type of digital product that you want to create.

Let's take a look at the four most popular choices in the market today:

E-books are by far and large the most popular digital products sold online.

All you really need to create an e-book is a great idea and Microsoft Word or any word processing program.

E-books are easy enough to create and don't necessarily take too much time to finish if you're familiar with the topic you're covering. It's also recommended that you deliver the finished product in PDF format, so that it's accessible across more platforms.

Video Tutorials can be done as live recordings or onscreen guides. Video tutorials about yoga, meditation, finance, entrepreneurship and online tools like WordPress and Google AdWords are especially popular. If you're filming a live action video tutorial, you want to ensure that you have adequate lighting and a good microphone - sound quality is something that should never be overlooked, even if you're doing an onscreen guide. Try to take your time when recording the video – you don't want to rush through something, leaving your viewer unable to catch up or hear what you are saying.

PowerPoint or Keynote slides are also a hit online – they're great for making information easy to digest. You don't need fancy animations – in the best of cases, presentation slides are not cluttered with too much text and aren't graphic-heavy. This is so that the slides are easy to read and don't take too long to load. You could even turn your slides into a video presentation. Just create your slides, write your transcript and get a voice over artist to record your transcript for each slide. You can then market your product as a bundle – this will increase the perceived value of your product.

Software might not be as easy to produce as e-books, slides and videos, but that doesn't mean they aren't worth the effort. There's a huge amount of cash to be made through well-made software. If you have an idea for software but don't have the technical know-how to create it, you can always outsource the job to a developer. It might take longer to create, but it's also something which you can sell at a higher price.

Of course, there are other types of digital products which you can choose to create – sets of graphics, photo collections, audiobooks, MP3 files and more. The sky's the limit.

But before you get started, do ask yourself which of these types of digital products would appeal more to your prospects. While you might be thinking of creating an e-book, maybe your target market would benefit more from a step-by-step video tutorial?

Maybe you're dealing in the Personal Development niche, where a guided meditation video would do the job more effectively than, say, a PowerPoint or Keynote slide presentation.

Crafting High-Selling Content

Now, it's time to craft the content that you are selling. As mentioned previously, specificity and focus can really make or break your launch.

To honor this, you need to pick topic and title that is focused. Vague titles don't sell well because they don't tell your prospects what they're in for. For example, would you rather buy a book titled "Money Online" or a book that proclaims "Make $10,000 A

Month With Internet Marketing"?

The second title is likely to sell better for a number of reasons - it very clearly tells people what they can accomplish, how long it takes and how they'll do it. "Money Online" is too generic to really pull people in because it doesn't give people a reason to purchase your product. In comparison, making 10,000 dollars a month is a pretty compelling reason for someone to buy your product.

On top of this, most products that sell really well are timely or immediately relevant and practical. This is content which speaks to people's wants and needs NOW rather than later.

For example, if there is a huge convention or expo concerning your niche coming up soon, people will want to brush up on their booth managing and networking skills before the event. If you were to launch an e-book a month before the event about

"Getting Your Booth Noticed at So & So Expo", chances are that many people would find value in your content and be compelled to make a purchase. This is because they can see exactly how this book can help them and they put what they learn to good use immediately.

This is why planning your launch schedule and doing significant market research is very important. You can close thousands of sales with this type of content – granted that you cater to your target market's urgent demands.

There are some categories of content which have proven to be highly profitable but it really depends on who you are targeting. "How To" guides and beginner's guides have proven to be a hot sell, regardless of niche or industry. Content that highlights the dos and don'ts of a niche are popular for beginners and intermediates as well.

You could also create content that is very heavily technical or requires advanced knowledge on the subject matter. This type of content usually zooms in on a very specific topic– for example, "How To Manually Install and Set Up WordPress". Though it may seem more advanced, this type of material has a good market standing – especially in the IM and Tech niches, where veterans are always seeking to improve.

PLR Content

Sometimes, it can take a lot of time to get a product ready for launch – from technical glitches to writer's block, there a bunch of external causes that can delay your product creation efforts. Luckily, you don't have to create your own product if you don't want to.

PLR stands for Private Label Rights. PLR products or content are products which, once purchased, you are legally allowed to manipulate, publish and re-sell as your own. That is to say, that when you purchase PLR content, you then own all or most of the intellectual property rights to the said work.

Usually, you can claim full authorship to a PLR product and you can make as many edits, changes and additions to these products as you see fit. The rights which you gain from PLR products varies from product to product so be sure to check the included rights before you make a purchase. Most websites that sell PLR content will provide a list of rights which come along with the purchase of each individual PLR product.

PLR products are great starting points if you don't want to create a product from scratch for your launch. They don't even cost very much to purchase – you can find e-books for under 5 US Dollars.

However, you should always double check the quality of the PLR product you are purchasing to make sure you're purchasing content which is marketable without you having to make too many edits in terms of fact-checking and grammar.

While you can just resell PLR products as is, it's highly recommended that you customize the product a little before reselling – think of it as rebranding. This will help to add value to your product so that your prospects will be more inclined to purchase it.

You'll find that most PLR products are relatively bare – e-books and slides tend to have little to no formatting or design. It's kept very black and white. You can consider adding a few headlines or maybe inserting one or two visuals, even adding a whole new chapter if you want to.

You might also want to curate content from more than just one PLR source –purchase 2 or 3 PLR e-books on your chosen topic instead of one. This way, you'll have more content and your end product will be more comprehensive.

You should also consider creating a new custom cover for your product – a bunch of other people might have bought the same PLR product and are reselling it as is, so you want yours to stand out and be perceived as different. Change the cover, change the headline and heavily edit. The point is to improve on quality.

While PLR products are purchased for really cheap, that doesn't mean that you have to sell your product for under 5 dollars as well – as you edit and breathe new life into the purchased PLR content, the value of the product increases. During your launch, if you've put together a good offer, you can charge a lot more – think double or triple.

Bottom line is, whether you started with a PLR product or if you did all the content creation yourself, you have to make the end product in your launch look like a custom, one of a kind product. It has to be a product which is tailored to a specific target market, stands out from the rest and has a high perceived value.

Sales Letter Formula

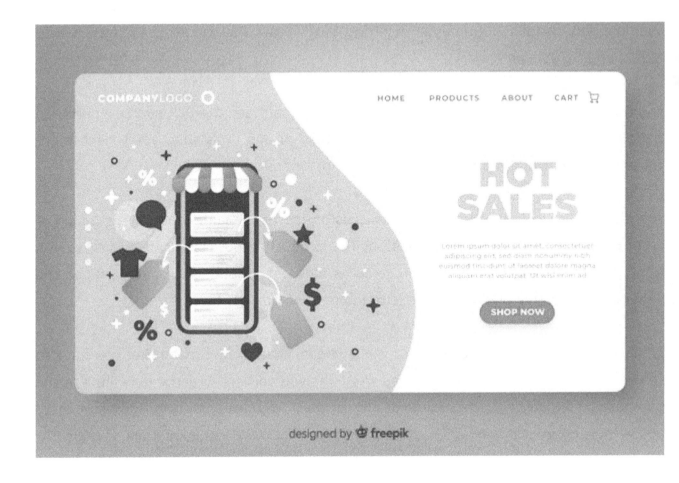

The sales letter is an integral part of internet marketing and typically takes the form of a webpage. During your product launch, its main purpose is to build interest and persuade your prospects to purchase your product. It's your 'pitch' to get them to click on your

Buy Button.

Types of Sales Letters

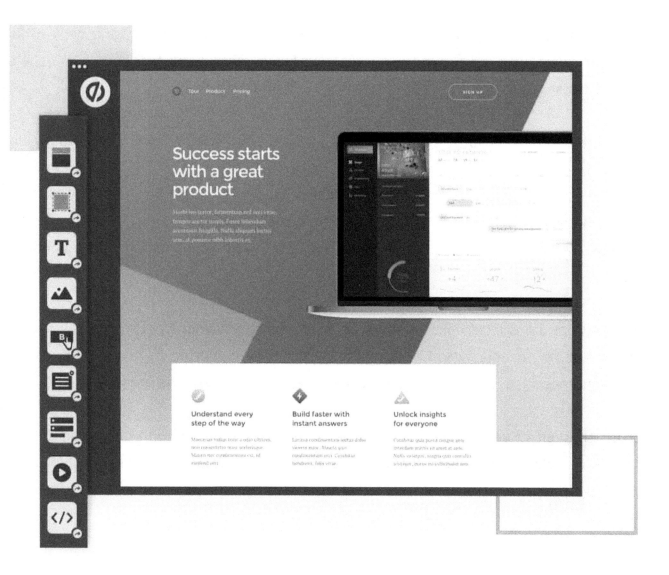

Let's take a look at the types of sales letters that you can construct for your product launch.

The Traditional Sales Letter - Pure Copy

While all sales letters focus on selling your product, a traditional sales letter is one which is primarily made up of text or copy, instead of graphics and visuals.

We call this sales letter format Pure Copy.

It doesn't contain any video and instead focuses more on its advertising copy. This form of sales letter may sound somewhat old-fashioned but the fact that this archaic method is still being used today is testament to its effectiveness.

While the copy is by far the core element of Pure Copy sales letters, they usually do contain some images and visuals of the product. Without them, a sales letter just wouldn't be complete. No matter how brilliant your copy might be, people work in a way whereby they need to see a product before purchasing it, so the use of product photos are still very important. However, in a Pure Copy sales letter, the visuals are used sparingly.

A Pure Copy sales letter focuses more on structure to entice prospects. What is meant by "structure", in this case, is not only how the copy is written in terms of language and sentence structure, but also the format in which information is presented.

It is very ineffective to have a sales letter that is strictly paragraph after paragraph of text – it makes information much harder to stomach. This is why Pure Copy Sales Letters make good, strategic use of bullet points, tables, and, as mentioned previously, visuals.

Pure Copy Sales Letters are great because full-page copy is less likely to have problems loading on your prospects' browsers. You could add a few photos to this Sales Letter and it should still load without error. This is compared to video sales letters, where heavier video files need to be uploaded and are more susceptible to error.

And no matter what, writing copy will always take less time than creating a video sales letter, so that's definitely a plus point to consider.

However, the Pure Copy format only truly works if you're good at writing copy. Because everything is so heavily reliant on your content, the sales copy has to be razor sharp and attention grabbing – which is harder than most people think.

The length of the copy is also something that needs to be looked at – if the copy runs on for too long, it's highly unlikely that your prospects will want to stay on your page and read on. Though, a fair amount of editing and a good copywriter would be able to help you fix these issues.

Video Sales Letters (VSLs) - 100% Pure

Another option for Sales Letters is to use video instead of copy. These types of sales letters are called pure video sales letters or Pure VSLs for short.

First of all, Pure VSLs are pages where there is only a video and an opt-in form or any other call-to-action. This is where the video does all the selling without the aid of text or copy. The page itself can usually be seen in whole without having to scroll down.

This kind of sales letter is more contemporary. Nowadays, communication has gotten more visual-heavy and Pure Video Sales Letters embody that change. A good Pure VSL should be direct and easy to navigate. Having that simplicity and directness prevents the page from being cluttered with copy, images, and unnecessary distractions. Often times, the prospect only needs to click the Play button on the video.

To make up for the absence of a copy in Pure VSLs, the script plays an important role. It may sound easy to write a script but, just like copywriting, it is an art of its own, so take some time with this or hire a writer to write one for you.

The presenter in the video, usually the product vendor, has to have a spokesperson's charm. All the qualities needed in face-to-face marketing are needed when you record a Pure VSL. Things like having a controlled tone of voice, clear and crisp pronunciation and a strong command of language play a big part in selling to your audience. Two other aspects to take note of are your body language (which people will read subconsciously) and your charisma, which you have to continuously build on.

The simple and modern design in most Pure VSLs helps make your page look more credible. A good video helps to boost your image in the eyes of your prospects as someone who is professional and takes their work seriously.

Also, a slick and clean design with a strong video presentation, has the power to be far more convincing than just copy. Your visitors do not have to read lengthy copy and can instead have you pitch to them, face- to-face, which makes it easier for visitors to absorb information.

As for drawbacks, there's a high risk of technical errors when it comes to a Pure VSL. If an error were to affect your video therefore making it unplayable or if someone on a weaker internet connection fails to load your video, there is nothing on your Pure VSL page that they can turn to. This is unlike a Pure Copy Sales Letters, whereby even if the images fail to load, your visitors would still be able to read your copy.

The Best of Both Worlds – Hybrid Sales Letter

If Pure Copy and Pure Video Sales Letters aren't your thing, why not try a Hybrid Sales Letter instead. A Hybrid Sales Letter is, essentially, a combination of both the Pure Copy Sales Letter and the Pure Video Sales Letter. In many ways, it has the best of both worlds.

A Hybrid Sales Letter has a sales video, which is usually the first thing the audience sees, at the top of the webpage. It is usually located directly below or above the headline. Unlike in Pure Copy Sales Letters, the headline is not the main attention grabber, though it is, of course, still important.

Underneath the video, you will have copy. It's important to note that this copy should NOT be a word for word transcript of your sales video. While you may reuse most of the information from your sales video (anywhere up to 90%), it's good to play around with the structure and phrasing. Try making the copy more reader-friendly with bullet points and formatting.

As for the length of the copy for the sales letter, it is entirely up to you. However, it's important to note here that the length of the copy is not the thing you should be most concerned about. A lot of people nitpick on being below a certain word count, when in fact, long form copy has proven to sell as effectively as short form copy.

One of the best reasons for choosing the Hybrid Sales Letter is that, as mentioned, it has the advantages of both Pure Video Sales Letter and Pure Copy Sales Letter.

The video allows your visitors to get all the offer information delivered to them in an easily digestible manner. They will not need to read through lengthy copy to find out what they need to know. On top of this, the video works as an attention-grabber and it is very effective in keeping the audience interested.

With the copy beneath the video, it also gives your prospects the option of reviewing your offer, without having to re-watch the video. The Hybrid Sales Letter basically gives your prospects the option of how they'd prefer to find out about your offer. This is why this sort of Sales Letter has become a popular choice for a lot of internet marketers today.

That said, there is a downside to using this type of sales letter – but it's not a big one.

With the Hybrid Sales Letter, you will have to do almost double the amount of work for your launch. On top of creating a video, you'll also have to spare some time to write the copy.

While it may seem time-consuming to create both video and copy, the rewards and success of your launch will make the effort worth it. Besides, you always have the option of delegating some of the work to creative professionals – sites like Fiverr are a great place for you to outsource tasks to capable creatives for cheap.

The Essential Formula

Your sales letter is so important – it does the bulk of the selling for you. A well-written and professionally produced sales letter truly is a vital aspect in your overall launch.

Below, you will find the formula for creating an amazing, irresistible Sales Letter. If you can effectively execute this formula, you will have a sales letter that is ready to go and create profit.

Know The Angle of Your Story

When you start your sales letter you need to come from a specific angle. Is this a real-life rags to riches tale? Is this a fictional or hypothetical story of what can happen to your prospects?

If your sales letter is a story, what you want to do is always end on a happy note, whereby the main character succeeds. A positive outcome is likely to put your prospects in a better mood and will motivate them to make a purchase. You should also include a cliffhanger in your story. Psychologically, humans crave closure. If you leave them with a cliffhanger or open loop, in terms of your sales letter, they will seek closure by continuing to read or listen to you.

The Who, What, When, Why, How

When it comes to writing your sales copy or creating your video sales letter, you need to give them important information about your product. Ideally, you should explain:

- who you are

- what you can do for your customers

- why they should purchase your product

- how they can follow up with you

- when they can expect results

Those are the bare essentials. Before you start working on anything else, make sure you get these points in your sales letter.

Bold Headline

A very important element that influences the effectiveness of a Sales Letter is the headline. At the end of the day, headlines determine whether the visitor will stay on your page and continue reading or move on to something else. You only have a very short period of time to engage a visitor that lands on your website. Make sure that your headline addresses their problem and offers a solution to it. It has to make a bold statement that entices your visitor to find out more.

Solving Problems

Be sure that your sales letter offers a solution to your prospects' challenges and problems. Reveal to them why most people have failed to get passed these obstacles. Then, you want to offer them a solution – let them know that you've experienced and overcome these challenges yourself and reassure them that they can do it too!

Features and Benefits

While it's important for you to promote your product and its features, you need to have accompanying benefits to help balance it out. Features are what your product can do. Benefits are what said features can do for your customer. In your sales letter, both of these should be 50-50. Remember – the sales page is meant to create interest in your visitors and you can only do that with a balance of information and persuasion.

Selling the dream

In your sales letter, you also want to focus on selling the dream. What you need to do is show your prospects how this product will not only solve their immediate problems, but also increase their happiness and improve on their quality of life. You need to get them passionate and enthusiastic about their own lives before they can be passionate and enthusiastic about what you are selling.

Put emphasis on bonus offers

When you create a product, you will also be creating a sales funnel. In this sales funnel, you will have upgrades and bonuses – like extension packs. Be sure to emphasize on these bonuses as these will be where the bulk of your profits will come from. Assure them that there is more to your offer than just a one off product.

Add Visual Elements

Photos and visuals of your product are really important when it comes to getting people to click on the buy button so make sure your graphics are clean and professional. At the same time though, you want to keep in mind to not flood your sales letter with too many images – they should complement, not overpower.

Build Credibility with Testimonials & Endorsements

You need testimonials! Without testimonials, you're just a person on the internet. With them, you build your credibility and establish yourself as someone who can be trusted and is capable of creating success stories. If you have big name joint venture partners, get them to write in as well to endorse your product. People need a reason to take your word and testimonials and endorsements will bring them one step closer to believing in you.

Include a Call to Action

You have just set up a great story with convincing points and have gotten your visitors interested. Now it's time for the final pull – assert a call to action. Guide them towards the action they need to take to get started with your product. Don't let them wonder whether they should click on the Buy button - tell them to do it.

How To Create Marketing Materials

Once you've set up your product and sales letter, you then need to move on to creating your marketing materials.

These are materials which will help you promote your launch and get sales from your followers. While you could run the gamut of marketing materials, there are two types of marketing materials which you should pay very close attention to; promotional e-mails and web banners.

Promotional E-mails

Promotional e-mails are what you use to promote your launch to your mailing list. It's the easiest way to tap into your leads and get sales, provided that your list has already been effectively built up.

You should start sending out these e-mails out a couple of weeks or at least a week before your projected launch date.

Expect to be sending out anywhere between 2 and 6 e-mails to your list during your pre-launch and launch period. This is so that you can steadily build hype with your prospects and start getting them interested.

While you can come up with the content for your e-mails from scratch, there are some e-mails which have proven to be very successful at enticing readers.

The Teaser

Teaser e-mails are usually the first promotional e-mails that you will send out to your list. Teaser e-mails are there to create curiosity and to hint at your newest product. The way you craft this e-mail is very important as you want to let them know that something big is coming, without saying what it is.

The point here is to not reveal too much – you want to tell them that you have something new coming up, something which you've been working on and are excited to share with them, but you don't want to mention specifics. Some people choose to send out two or three teaser e-mails during the pre-launch period.

Product Introduction

This is the e-mail that you will send out on your launch day. Let your prospects know that the product is now available online.

You can enclose the highlights of your product and its unique features. You should also include a link to the product's sales page and you can even state the price of your product but remember - this e-mail is NOT meant for you to start selling to them. It is for you to introduce the product and get their interest.

Benefits

This e-mail focuses on highlighting the benefits of your product. You want to tell your prospects what's in it for them if they purchase your product. Benefits are usually paired with features, but for the purpose of this e-mail, make the benefits the champion. You need to make these benefits compelling to your prospects – focus on how they can greatly improve their lives and help them reach end-goals. Sell the dream.

Additional Bonuses

The additional bonuses e-mail is a promotional e-mail which helps promote your other bonuses. As mentioned in previous modules, the bulk of profit from your launch will come from the sales you make via your sales funnel. Because of this, you should have a promotional e-mail dedicated to talking about your bonuses.

This e-mail doesn't just have to be about the expansion to your front-end product – it can also be about subscriber-only discounts. You want to let your prospects know that they have access to bonuses if and when they choose to get in on the bandwagon.

Bypassing Spam Filters

As with any form of writing, promotional e-mails require carefully curated information. However, the stakes are somewhat high with promotional e-mails – seeing as you will

be sending them en masse to your mailing list, if your e-mails aren't done right, they will just be flagged as spam by e-mail service providers.

To ensure that your promotional e-mails don't immediately end up in the junk folder, you should:

Have a Plain Text version if you're sending HTML e-mails

If you are using HTML for your promotional e-mails, ensure that you enclose a plain text version of your e-mail. This is a very effective way to prevent your e-mail from ending up in the junk folder. Also, some of your recipients may not be able to open HTML e-mails so this offers a solution to that problem, too.

Have a balance between graphics, links and text

Firstly: NEVER send graphic-only or link-only e-mails. You should always try to strike a balance between your graphics, links and text. While this is really up to your own discretion, you should try to avoid including graphics in your body copy altogether. But if you must, then ensure that the accompanying body copy text make ups at least 70% of your includinge-mail content. And as for links, you want to keep them minimal. Try only having between 2-4 links in your e-mail's body copy.

Pick attachments wisely

As a general rule, you want to avoid sending any executable attachments (.exe, .zip,

.swf, etc.) as these will likely cause your e-mail to go straight into the junk folder. JPEGs, GIFs, PNGs & PDFs are attachments which work best, as long as your e-mail body copy has text to back it up.

Subject Lines

Getting past the spam filters is one thing – getting sales with your promotional e-mails is a whole different ball game. In truth, the only way your promotional e-mails are going to be have a high open rate is if they are crafted with a strong subject line. You could have e-mailed thousands of leads in your list but if your subject line doesn't grab their attention and entice them to click on your e-mail, then all your work would be for naught.

Here are some easy tips which you can apply to your subject line to ensure your promotional e-mails get opened and make conversions!

Stay Away from Overused Sales Jargon

People never want to be sold to. They may like purchasing, but they hate being sold to.

Try staying away from words like "discount", "deal", "learn", "act now", "report" – the common words that are usually associated with sales and content marketing.

There's a very high chance that your prospects are subscribed to other mailing lists as well so your promotional e-mails aren't the only ones they receive. Imagine getting three e-mails in the same week (or day!) and all of them having the same sales jargon subject line.

Keep Subject Lines Short

Your subject lines should be short and crisp. When people open their e-mail inbox, they usually just scan through subject lines before deciding if an e-mail is worth reading. If your subject line has over 10 words, you need to chop it down. You could even use the popular 50 characters or less as a pointer. The easier it is for your prospects to read your subject line, the likelier they are to click "open".

Include an Action Word

An e-mail subject line should also act as a call-to-action. Including action words or verbs in your subject line tells your prospect that there's something for them to do. Most e-mails only require the recipient to read through copy – having an actionable subject line is way more exciting and creates a sense of urgency. It also sets them up for taking action later on – whether it's clicking on a link in your e-mail or downloading a file.

Banner Ads

Promotional e-mails help you spread word of your launch to your list but how about the people who aren't on your list? If you have an active website or other webpages, there's a stream of traffic that you can tap into. All you need are banner ads.

Banner ads are a form of online advertising. Web banners are embedded into a web page and serve as advertisements. They are intended to divert traffic to a specific website. When it comes to product launches, banner ads are usually linked to your sales page or sales letter.

You can also share your banners with your affiliates, so that they can use it on their sites and landing pages, as tools to promote your product launch. With banner ads, you get to make the most out of the web traffic that you and your joint venture partners receive on a daily basis.

Banner Elements

What elements should you include in your banner? Well, you should definitely display your product name – have it bolded or use a larger font size to help it stand out.

If you have a product photo, put that in there as well as visuals tend to attract more clicks. If you don't have a product photo, a logo will do. Just make sure that it is displayed in full view without any obstructions.

If your banner size allows it, you can even have a sentence in the banner highlighting a strong benefit that your product offers. However, you don't want to cramp your banner ad with too much text. So, you should only include this when you have the space to accommodate it.

Another very vital element that you need to have is a Call to Action button. This should be a clickable button that links to your product's sales page. The text on the button can read "Buy Now" or "Get it now" or "Learn More" – it's completely up to you.

Banner Design

As for the overall design, we would recommend that your banner ads follow the color scheme of your product's sales page or whatever page your Call To Action button links to. There's nothing more off-putting than clicking on a link that directs you to a page that looks completely different from what you had in mind.

Keep the layout clean and uncluttered, with a flat design. Flat designs are more appealing nowadays and a loud, flashy banner ad is now seen as unappealing to the general masses.

Banner Sizes

Now that you know the important elements of a successful banner ad, it's time to choose your banner sizes. Generally, you want to have at least 3 to 5 different-sized

banner ads designed. Because you'll be sharing these banners with your affiliate network, you never know which sizes of banners would work best on their own websites, so it's good to offer variation.

If you're unsure of what banner sizes to choose, here are some common banner sizes which you may want to look into. You can also look online for the list of standard banner sizes to find the ones which suit you and your affiliate network best.

• 250x250 pixel banners are sometimes referred as "square pop-ups". Banners of this size are great for pop ups.

• 728x90 pixel banners are known as "leaderboards". These work best when they are placed at the top of a webpage. It offers lots of usable space.

• 160x600 pixel banners or, "wide skyscrapers", work best when they are placed along the sidebars of webpages. These types of banners are good at accommodating product images.

• 336x280 pixel banners are also called "large rectangles". You can usually use these ate the bottom corners of webpages or at the end of articles.

• 300x600 pixel banners are known as "half page". Gives you lots of space to play around with. Usually placed along the edges of webpages.

Sales Funnel Secrets For Earnings Per Click (EPC)

What Happens in Your Sales Funnel?

Awareness — Brand • Marketing Activities

Leads — Create • Squeeze Pages • Opt-in Offers

Prospects — Content • Email Follow-ups • Offers

Sales — Build • Memberships • Loyalty Programs • Customer Specials

Loyal Customers

Over the last few decades, Internet marketing has evolved with lightning speed. In the beginning of the internet business era, a business could still sustain long term profit if it only produced and sold one high-priced product. However, following the huge changes in the nature of these businesses, relying on only one product isn't enough to keep your business alive anymore.

Despite all the changes, people continue to strive for success. In this chapter, I am going to show you the secret technique that changes the fate of Internet businesses – the Sales Funnel. This is the secret technique that all the other Internet marketers use to increase their Earnings Per Click (EPC).

It might not sound special now to some of you, but you will definitely fall in love with this technique when you see how it can bring massive wealth to your business.

With the implementation of a sales funnel, you can increase your revenue without putting in extra effort for extra traffic. The Sales Funnel is a proven technique, so you need not to worry about whether it works or not. Sales funnels are a time-tested technique.

When you apply a sales funnel into your launch, it will definitely be your main stream of income. And you will be able to see the results almost instantly. Without further ado, let's get started.

The Sales Funnel Formula

Now that you already know how amazing a sales funnel is, there is no reason for you to not incorporate a Sales Funnel into your launch. Below, you will find the Sales Funnel formula. Of course, after years of experience in the Internet business, this is the most ideal model that increases revenue. Let's get down to each of the steps in the formula.

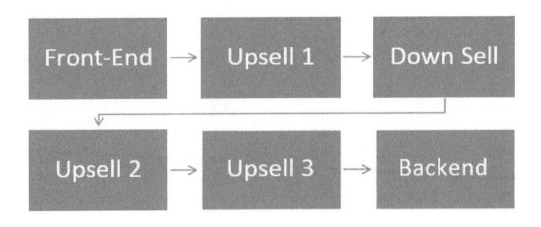

Front-End

As you can see from the diagram above, the sales funnel starts with a front-end product. This will be the first product, or what is sometimes known as a frontline product, which your potential customer will see.

Your front-end product will be sold at a cheaper price ranged from $7 to $10. Even though the front-end sells at a cheaper price, it doesn't mean that you can put lesser attention to this. Without a great front-end product, the whole sales funnel will be affected.

Front-end products can be said to be the most important product in your sales funnel because it represents the first impression to your potential customers. The perceived value of your launch will depend on the front-end product.

is is especially important if you are a newbie in the Internet business - the front-end product is the product that will build up your credibility along the way. If the quality of the front-end is not up to standard, what more about the other products?

A front-end product also serves as a catalyst for a buying frenzy. After someone makes their first purchase, they will not be aware of how much more they are willing to spend.

Imagine this scenario: You've prepared a shopping list before you go grocery shopping, but you still end up buying more than you've planned to buy. Does this sound familiar to you?

This is exactly how sales funnels work. When you've already started spending money, it becomes natural for you to say yes to other offers and spend more money than you initially intended.

Upsells

Moving on, you might've noticed that there are 3 upsells included in the flowchart. If I tell you that these upsells are the main source of revenue in the sales funnel, you would not think that 3 upsells are enough. But, do not worry - you will put a higher price tag for your upsells, anywhere in the range of $20-$50 is a good starting point.

While front-end will initiate the buying frenzy, upsells are an immediate offer after your front-end product, so that they can continue and prolong the buying frenzy. This is why your first upsell must be an offer that is too good to refuse – it plays a very important role in keeping the buying frenzy alive and well.

Your upsell offer can be an advanced solution or follow-up from your front-end offer. For instance, if your front-end product is about how to build and grow a mailing list, your upsell may be another training course to teach them how to direct massive traffic to the website.

This would be a great offer because the next thing an Internet marketer needs after the setup of a landing page is traffic. This will be a solution for the forecasted problem which is why you can scale the price of your upsell. Just think of upsells as upgrades and add-ons for the front-end product.

A small tip: Offer bonuses in your upsell one. While the offering of a solution for forecasted problems is a good angle, adding in a bonus will increase the perceived value of your upsell.

As you can see after the down sell, the sales funnel is then continued with another two upsells. Always keep in mind that the whole sales funnel must be congruent – meaning all the products fit in harmony.

The upsell 2 and upsell 3, obviously, must be something related to the front-end. So, when you are planning out your Sales Funnel, you must pick on a few related sub-topics to focus your upsell. This is how you draft a great Sales Funnel.

Downsell

As mentioned previously, a downsell happens after the first upsell. In downsell, you'll remove the bonuses and re-offer them the same upsell product but this time at a lower price.

Some of the buyers may be hesitant to purchase the first upsell. And when this happens, right after they've clicked on the 'No Thanks' button, they will be redirected to a downsell.

Remove all the bonuses you offered in the first upsell and give them another chance to reconsider the offer. They may be hesitant to purchase the first upsell because of the price or they may be having second thoughts because they don't think the upsell is worth the price.

So, here's when down sell comes in as a discount for the same product without bonuses. Take note of removing the bonuses because this is very important. If you did not remove the bonuses and offer the same offer in lower price, it would be unfair for the people who purchased your first upsell.

Backend

The final product in the Sales Funnel is called a backend product. Usually the offers in your launch will end at the third upsell. The backend offer will happen only after a few days in the follow-up emails.

The reason is because backend product can be a long term coaching program or membership sites that can be priced up to $997. Imagine if you suddenly offer the buyers a product in such high price, chances that they will consider this offer are lower.

You wouldn't want to scare them away by putting this up first. After they've read through or ran through your training courses, the trust they put in your will be higher. This is the right timing when you can offer them the backend.

So, you must remember to put your backend offer in the follow up emails a few days after they've purchased your product. The backend offer is an optional step for your prospects who are interested.

Some of the marketers might not have a backend product to offer. The higher price the product is, the higher the expectation from the customers. So, if you do not have a backend to offer them yet, do not rush in to offer them a lower quality one.

This is very dangerous as this can ruin your reputation.

Earnings Per Click (EPC)

In the beginning of this chapter, I've mentioned that sales funnels are the secret technique that all the other Internet marketers use to increase their Earnings Per Click, or in short EPC. I will elaborate and explain about EPC and will introduce the formula to calculate it, too.

EPC is the average earnings of each click that your affiliates and/or you send to your website. It involves your conversion rate so if your EPC on average is $2 and above, you are doing good.

EPCs Formula

How do you calculate your EPC? The formula of EPC is:

EPC =

I want you to picture this scenario: Let's say you are able to direct hundred clicks to your website regardless from your own traffic or your affiliates. And from these 100 clicks, two of them made purchase of a product worth $50.

So, the formula will be:

EPC =   = 1

50 times 2, which is your sales, the money you've made. And then sales divided by the number of clicks. What you make from sales here is $100 divided by the number of clicks, which are 100 clicks.

Your EPC, in this case, would be $1.

For bigger picture of EPC, let's go through it with another example. If you direct 300 clicks to the website, and 8 of them make purchase of a $100 product, your sales would be $800.

So, put all the elements in to the formula:

EPC =   = 2.67

After dividing, you'll get $2.67. That amount is the EPC. Not so hard after all. As long as you remember the formula, put every elements in to the formula, you can do the math too.

In a nutshell...

The implementation of a sales funnel in to your launch increases the chance to boost your sales. When your sales are high, it directly increases the EPC of your launch.

In conclusion, a higher product's EPC reflects higher sales in your launch. It is more likely to get a higher rank in Search Engine Optimization (SEO) with a higher EPC because it reflects that the traffic to your website is high, too.

Even though it sounds like a great idea to make as much sales as possible by directing more traffic to your website, but it is not wise to send traffic randomly.

You need to know who the product's target market is and who is in the niche. Sending in random traffic, indeed, can increase the conversion rate, but it will not increase the sales.

This is the basic rule of marketing that applies in all business. Remember, all traffic must be targeted traffic.

How To Win The Joint Venture

A Joint Venture (JV) is a great way to promote and sell your product. Its reach can go really viral and messages can get across conveniently, because with the help of Joint Ventures, you reach the people who you initially couldn't reach.

When you are launching your product, it is fine to have a smaller list to start with.

However, once you've successfully launched a few products, you would want to grow your business.

A Joint Venture is the most effective way to do this. With Joint Ventures, you can make great impressions in the market and grow your list easily. JVs are the affiliates that help a product vendor, which is you in this case, to promote the launch.

In return of the favor of the affiliates promoting the launch, the vendor will pay the affiliates in terms of commission.

You may be wondering what exactly the differences between JVs and affiliates are. Actually, they are pretty much the same, but JVs usually have a closer relationship with you. That is basically the only difference between a JV and affiliate.

After some time of networking in the Internet business, you usually will have a closer relationship with the affiliates that help you to promote your launch. Especially for those who always work with you.

There may be a chance for you to launch a product together with your affiliates. After some time of knowing each other, you'll not call them just an affiliate anymore. They become your Joint Venture partners.

With the help of the JVs, you can easily boost the sales in your launch. Because a JV's commission is based on their results, they work hard to earn their pay. This ensures a wider reach. Really, it's a great way to expand your Internet business.

Like I said, you will get instant result with JVs. How? Well, say if you have 10 JV partners, with thousands of subscribers in each of their list. It makes up tens of thousands of subscribers collectively.

Once you give them the promotional tools, your offer will be mailed out to that amount of subscribers in their list! Isn't this amazing? You get to reach out to the people that you initially couldn't. The best part is that you will get in touch with them soon, too.

This works especially if you work with JVs who have a mammoth of subscribers list. They can bring in massive traffic to your website in no time.

Speaking of JVs with massive lists, this is also a plus for you. JVs with massive list are often credible and trusted, which is why they have that much reach. While their subscribers already know that your JVs can be trusted, they will know that you are a trusted source as well!.

The request for them to opt-in to your mailing list would be easier. Meaning, you get to add more e-mail addresses to your own list as well.

The advantages of getting JVs into your launch will not stop here. When you are getting them to your launch, believe it or not, it will not cost you a single cent - the expense is $0.

You do not have a take out any money to form a joint venture with them. As mentioned, your payment for them will be the commission, which means, you are paying them based off their performance.

When a front-end product is sold, 100% of the money will go to them. You do not really need to worry about the risks because you are not taking any risk at all.

If you've convinced an influential affiliate to be part of your launch, your promotion has the potential to reach to a massive group of people. Hence, you will have the chance of converting a very, very high number of sales.

This is possible with only one affiliate. Think about what if you have approached 10 others of this caliber? Don't be afraid to ask for joint venture. After all, you don't have to pay for their service.

Joint Venture Commission Rates

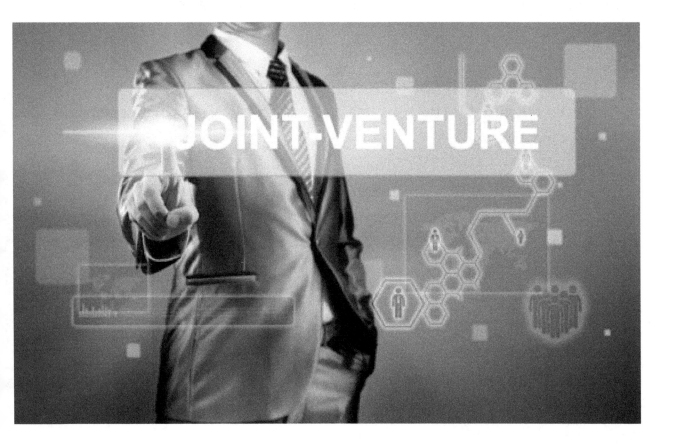

What are the commission rates that JVs usually receive? The commission rates are up to the vendors to decide so you will have the full control on the rate.

Bear in mind that the rate of the commission will affect the decision of affiliates on whether to promote your product or not. This being said, if the vendors set a rate that is not really intriguing, it's less likely that they will get any affiliates to participate in the affiliate program.

When affiliates arrive in the affiliate invitation page, the first thing an affiliate will be looking for is 'What's in it for me'. This is an important point that I must stress on, because this can be applied to almost all situations.

When you are writing the affiliate invitation page or sales page, always remember what people want to know. They will stay longer for the pages that can tell them what they want to know.

Back to the affiliate commission rates – you want to set the best rates that are agreeable by the affiliates. Here are the commission rates, which are commonly used by Internet marketers:

- Front-end: 100%

- Upsell:

o $297 – 50% o $497 – 40% o $997 – 30%

For the front-end product, you can afford to pay them a 100% commission. Really, give out the full payment of your front-end to the JVs. Do not worry about giving it all out, because the main stream of revenue doesn't comes from the front-end anyway.

When a customer makes a purchase, they will be directed through a sales funnel, as you already know that by now. The revenue comes from the upsells and backend in the sales funnel. As for higher ticket products, however, it varies. There is no hard and fast rule here so you can always change the rates accordingly. What I am going to show you is just a reference.

You will not want to give 100% commissions for this. So, if you are selling a $297 product, give out 50% of it; $497 product for 40%; and lastly $997 product for 30%. In the end, the commission rate is still up to you.

However, keep in mind the 'What's in it for me' concept. It is best that you always set an agreeable commission rate. The affiliates deserve what they work for.

How To Find Joint Venture Partners

Now that you know that JVs can be a powerful arsenal to make sales, but the next thing you may be wondering is where do you go to find them? There are many ways. And if it works, it's not wrong. There are always places where you can find all the JVs. Here, I'll show you the best places to find JVs.

Social Media Platforms

The first place to go for is, without doubt, the social media platforms. It is the easiest way to find people, because most people are more active on social networks such as Facebook and Twitter than checking their emails.

For Facebook, you can start by requesting to join Internet marketers' groups. Some of the groups may be a closed group, where you may need to wait for the approval from the admin. But good things deserve your time investment. Once you've gotten the approval, join their group discussions to build up a relationship with them. Ask questions, answer questions, give feedback – all that jazz.

Most importantly, you do all these to make yourself visible in the group. If you are to build a long term relationship with them, start with offering to promote their launch first. This way, it is easier to ask for a favor to promote your launch in the future.

In addition, when you make the first move to approach them, they are more likely to have a better impression towards you.

Joint Venture Broker

Another way to find JVs is to go to a JV broker. JV brokers usually already have the connection to other Internet marketers in the business. They serve the role as the bridge among Internet marketers and, sometimes, they are Internet marketers themselves.

For a fee, they will help you to find JVs. This will make your job much easier, as they already have a list of Internet marketers. You have to give them the criteria such as the niche, size of mailing list, and so on.

And then, they will match the criteria to the Internet marketers they have on hand. If you are a newbie in this business, this is the easier way to get you connected with other marketers.

This not only makes your job easier, but it will also make your promotion stronger.

However, there's still a fee to be paid as mentioned. But with the results that good JVs bring, it's an investment worth making.

Live Events

If there is live networking event around your area, do not hesitate to attend the event. If it is convenient for you, go ahead for the networking session, because this is a great way to find JVs.

If you ever want to take your online business up a level or two, you should always be ready to network. No one in the Internet business goes alone. Always remember that networking is of the utmost importance to grow your Internet business and the results that networking brings are definitely worth your time.

You must be active in networking events, because when you meet the affiliates face-to-face, instead of communicating through emails or Skype, they are more likely to be excited by the prospect of your business.

Chances will be higher to convince them to form a joint venture with you. If there is opportunity for you to join live events, don't hesitate and march right on.

Subscribe to New List

Lastly, you can find affiliates by actually subscribing to their mailing list first. When you

join the list, you can see how they do their promotions, what kind of tone they use to sell, and what kind of products do they sell and promote.

This would be a great opportunity to evaluate their approach. If the approach and niche suit your culture, you can then consider approaching them.

How to Pull Off a Successful Joint Venture Invitation

After you've found the JVs you want to approach, how do you pull off a successful JV invite? It's no walk in the park, but it's not that difficult, either.

JVs will be interested in your business if you have a really good product and affiliate offers for them. You also have to play your cards right.

Quite a number of factors that will attract an affiliate to join your program, and it's all up to them. But, in the core of it all, is the 'What's in it for me', which I've mentioned a few times before this.

In order to pull off a successful JV invite, you must provide a solution that leads to a win-win situation. Most importantly, provide a high commission rate for them. This is usually the first thing a JV is looking for in the affiliate page.

Sometimes, they look at the product. If you can give complimentary access to your product, it will be a plus for them. When they have the access to your product, they will have an opportunity to evaluate your product before they promote your launch.

This way, they can ensure the quality of the product that they are going to promote and make sure what they're promoting is a product good enough for their subscribers. If you are confident in your product, the affiliates will be confident, too.

But essentially, the numbers are important too! To win them, provide a high commission rate. After all, there are no fast and hard rules in setting up the commission rate.

Next, affiliates are also often attracted to a contest. There are quite a number of affiliate contests you can find in the marketplaces. Whichever affiliate generates the most sales, wins.

The winner usually gets reward in monetary form. This would be an extra incentive for them. What is so great about an affiliate contest is that on top of having paid in commissions, they stand a chance to win a bonus.

As mentioned, to get affiliates, you must first be an affiliate. Demonstrate your value by promote their launch first. You will establish a business relationship with the affiliate before asking them to do a joint venture.

When you offer a favor first, it is easier to ask for a favor from them! You can't be blunt here so show them your value first. They will appreciate the gesture of you doing a favor for them first.

Joint Venture Page for Affiliates

Once the affiliates have agreed to join your affiliate program, the next thing you need is a JV page for the affiliates. This is where the affiliates go to register their affiliation with you.

In this page, you should provide an opt-in box to collect their name, email and marketplace IC such as from JVZoo or ClickBank. This is to ensure they have applied to your affiliate program.

They will need to opt-in in order to get their affiliate link from you. And your job as the vendor is to approve their request to be your affiliate. However, if you already have some trusted JVs, you can put them under the auto-approve list.

For your information, when you are in the Internet business long enough, you may be getting affiliate requests every now and then. You get to choose the status for that particular affiliate, which are deny, delayed, instant and auto-approve.

A small guide for you in choosing the status for your affiliate:

- 0-50: Delayed

- 50 and above: Instant

Like I said, the auto-approve applies to the trusted JVs. Denies seldom happen, unless there is special case where you already know that affiliate request is a scam.

In this page also, you must provide the promotional tools for the JVs. This is necessary, as the JVs would need some tools to promote your product.

Such as graphics, swipe emails, and so on. Here, you can include any other promotional tool that you think is fitting like a video, for example. It's best that you provide them sufficiently.

Launch Time

If you make it through all the processes that you need to walk through before the launch, congratulations. You are now just a step away from your launch.

Here we come to a chapter about your launch time. Launch day is the day where you will reap what you've sowed from the beginning; it is the day you've been building toward. It is very hard to describe the excitement on your launch day.

In this chapter, I am going to show you the whole process before your launch and walk you through step-by-step to make sure everything is all good to go.

Without further ado, let's get into it.

3-Step Launch Plan

Here's a 3-step launch plan for you. Of course, it is not a simple task to be accomplished without putting in any effort. But, it is not hard either. All you need to do is to double check everything and make sure everything is good to go.

Create a checklist and ensure everything in the checklist is fine. This way, you can prevent any last minute changes and put on the show perfectly.

#1: Set your date and time ahead

First, obviously, you need to set your date and time. You can, of course, prepare the launch without a date and time in the first place. However, if you have a goal to achieve, you will be motivated to finish the job on time.

It is also better to have a date and time set beforehand so you can prepare your promotional emails in advance. You can then upload the follow-up email series to your autoresponder and do other important tasks.

There is a myth about the best days to launch a product, which falls on Tuesday and Wednesday. According to researchers, people are usually free to attend to a product launch on Tuesday and Wednesday, because those are the days where their work isn't that busy.

While Monday is too soon after the weekend and people are still getting settled in to work, Thursday and Friday are too close to the weekend. Therefore, Tuesday and Wednesday will be the best days.

However, I believe that whether you launch it on any of the best days of the week or not, as long as you have mailed out the launch date and time ahead to your list, any day is a good day to launch. Do not let this myth limit your plan.

#2: Pre-launch campaign

Next, you will need to make sure the pre-launch campaign runs smoothly. The pre-launch is essential. Pre-launch is the process where you will announce your launch date and time to your subscribers.

In the pre-launch, the promotional emails that you send to your subscribers are to stir up the excitement. Let them know there will be something special and new for them coming up soon.

I want you to imagine this scenario: When you are informed that next Wednesday is going to be a holiday, won't you start looking forward to the holiday? No matter how small the excitement is, you are already excited for the holiday that is coming soon.

Same goes for when you inform your subscribers ahead of your launch time. They will feel the excitement as well, because they know something good is going to happen soon.

In the pre-launch campaign, the first thing you need to attend to will be the sales page. As mentioned in the previous chapter, sales page is the first page your subscribers will see and is also the link that you will attach in your promotional email.

While promotional emails serve as a pre-sell to the subscribers, a sales page is the main page – the call-to-action page. Most of the Internet marketer put most of their effort into the sales page, because whether the product is going sell like a hot cake or not depends mostly on the sales page.

However, do not turn your sales page into a 'Buy my stuff! Buy my stuff!' page. Always remember this: People do not like to be sold, but they like to buy. There are ways to entice them.

So, make sure your sales page is good to go. Check on all the elements in the sales page such as headline, videos, graphics, call-to-action, and many more. Not to be paranoid, but double or even triple check your sales page.

Setting up your sales page will be especially important because the sales page will make the first impression to your subscribers and at the same time, the sales page affects the decision of your subscribers.

Whether they will click on the buy button and check out for your product, or click on the leave button, it is all depends on your sales page.

Here's an additional step, you can conduct a split-test for your sales page. Sometimes, a simple tweak will make a huge different. It can be the choice of words you use in your headline; it can be the price you set; it can be the color scheme. You will know what works best when you conduct a split test.

However, you will change only one or two elements each time you conduct a split test, so that you will know which element to improve on for your next launch. Choose the best conversion page as your sales page.

Moving on, the next thing you need to do is create your ad campaign in social media platforms like Facebook and Twitter. Like I said, social media platforms will be the best place to promote your launch, as most of the people are more active in social media than checking their emails.

Especially for newbies, once you've set up your own fan page, you might need to build up your followers through buying ads from Facebook or Twitter. Once you've built up a large pool of followers, you can then post your offer without buying ads.

Other than the fan page, you can join the groups related to your niche. When you post an ad in such groups, you are getting the targeted audience in your niche. This way, you do not need to worry about getting people that you don't want into your list.

Lastly, contact the JVs and mail out to your own list. The nearer the launch date is, the more you need to keep in touch with your JVs to mail out your offer.

Contact your JVs to follow up on the progress in promoting your launch, or sending a reminder to send the promotional emails ahead to announce the launch date.

This is not a compulsory move, as your JVs know what they need to do for the launch. However, it is good to contact your JVs before the launch, to build up relationship with them as well as to keep track on the details of your launch.

I would like to mention about this one more time; the promotional emails are really crucial as it is going to be what will build up the excitement. So, do not be hesitant to contact the JVs to make sure everything runs smoothly according to your plan.

And, of course, do not forget about your own list. As mentioned, you can set your promotional e-mails in advance with your autoresponder. When you do this, you don't need to worry about mailing out your emails to your list and can focus on other parts of your marketing. Autoresponders will mail out your offer to your subscribers accordingly.

#3: Launch strategy

And then, plan your launch strategy on your launch day. Different kinds of strategies bring you different kinds of results. Be sure what kind of technique you want to use in your launch to enhance your call-to-action. It is important to decide on the launch strategy that you are going to use for your launch. This can be an enhancement to build up a stronger call-to-action.

First, you can set a period of time for the offer. For instance, price goes up after certain period of time, or bonuses will be removed when the promotion is over. When there is a time limit for something, people tend to have lesser time to make decision. It somehow acts as a catalyst to speed up the time they take to make a decision. Create a sense of urgency, whereby they need to make a fast decision - either buy now or never. This is one of the strategies you can use for your launch. I am going to talk about other techniques you can apply in your launch in the next chapter. Stay tuned for that! During the launch, you can still mail out to your list. Sometimes, we stop mailing out to the subscribers after the launch. Indeed, you can still mail out during the launch to make a final call for your launch.

You first email can be a social proof email, to further convince them to take action; Second email can be a short Q & A email, to tell them what your product is; Third email can be a reminder that you are going to close your promotion offer to them, to stir up the sense of urgency. If the offer is going to last for a week, send them one email every two days.

Product Launch Techniques

To conduct a successful launch that brings massive income, product launch techniques are what you will definitely fall in love with! These are the techniques that all Internet marketers implement in their launch.

Meaning to say, all these techniques are time-tested techniques which are guaranteed to bring massive revenue to your launch.

Most of the product launch techniques create a sense of urgency for your prospects to buy from you. They create a sense that if they don't buy from you, they will miss the chance to join in on something great.

You can use these techniques individually in the beginning. But once you are familiar with the techniques, you can always mix and match the techniques and form your own marketing strategy.

Test out the techniques - you may be surprised by the results you get almost instantly. Just a small change makes a huge different to your launch's success.

With the implementation of product launch techniques, you could easily gain at least 10% more sales. Without sending extra traffic or putting in more effort to sell, these techniques will do the magic for you. Let's get down to the techniques now!

#1: Bonuses

The first technique is to offer bonuses in your first upsell offer. Once you've successfully convinced them to buy the front-end from you, you have already created a buying frenzy in them. Don't let the loop end here. The first upsell offer must be another no-brainer offer that should be grabbed.

What can you do to turn this upsell offer into another no brainer offer to grab? The upsell must be something congruent to the front-end, such as an immediate solution for forecasted problems.

The perceived value of an upsell is already high. So, when you offer them the upsell with the bonuses, it doubles the value of the offer. You must always remember that when you are preparing the sales funnel; every product in the loop must be congruent to each other, including the bonuses. Imagine this: What is the feeling when you see the sales page of an Internet marketing product bundled with an infographic product as a bonus? It feels weird, huh? You don't want to have your prospects feel this way so always remember to plan the sales funnel properly.

#2: Discount

Everyone loves discount. Giving out discount offers for your front-end product is another technique. You can implement the price slashing technique here.

State the original price of the product, slash it off and replace it with the price after discount. As you already know, visuals always work better than just words and numbers.

Other than using the price slashing technique, you can set a period of time for the discount offer to create a sense of urgency as mentioned in the previous chapters. With a shorter time to consider the offer, they are more likely to grab the offer.

Here's a tip for you: Create a countdown timer in the page. This way, you need not emphasize on the discount offer in your sales letter, the countdown timer does it all for you.

#3: Scarcity

Scarcity is one of the most powerful mental triggers where you put limitations in your launch. What a scarcity factor does is it creates an invisible 'force' to shorten their time in making a decision about your product. This is a strong call-to-action. When you limit the number of your items, they will have lesser time to think. There has to be some negative consequences if they don't take the offer quickly. You have nothing to lose in this case. So, do not be afraid to use this technique. The theory why this technique works is really simple, "When there is less of something, we want it more". It is this simple. Try this technique now and see how this brings your business up to a completely different level. If you are familiar with HTML, you can make a counter to countdown the number of your items, too!

#4: Dime Sale

Finally, the last technique that I am going to lead you through is the dime sale technique. A dime sale is a technique where you will increase the price of your product with each purchase made.

Dime sale is a really powerful mental trigger as well. This technique is tenser than all the other techniques. It creates an even stronger force to motivate potential buyers to make the decision to buy right away, because if they don't buy now, the price will not be the same anymore.

To plan out this technique, you will need to set a starting and finishing price and, of course, the price increment per sale. For instance, let say the starting price for your front-end is $7. The price goes up $1 each time a purchase made. Finally, the sales will be ended when the price hit $15.

This is just an example to show you how exactly dime sale can be done. You can plan out yours as well!

Affiliate Marketing For Beginners

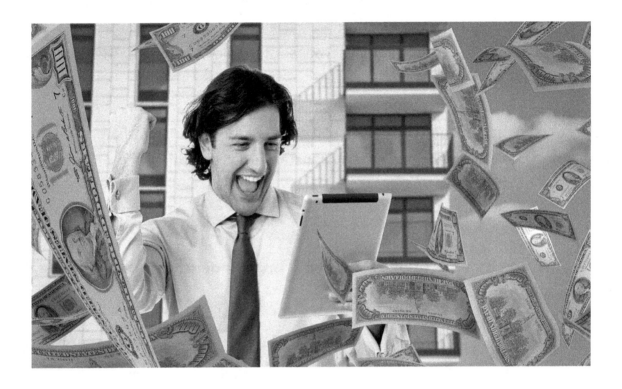

The most popular way to make money online fast.
You look for a product that you like,
promote it to others and earn a part of the profit
from each sale that you make.

(<u>BONUS 2</u>) – FREE BOOK - By : "Santiago Johnson Smith"

TABLE OF CONTENTS [BONUS 2 - AFFILIATE MARKETING FOR BEGINNERS]

Yahoo and MSN's Adwords Equivalent Contextual Advertising

Facebook and Myspace Advertising

Squidoo and Hubpages

Web 2.0 Social Networking

The Advantages of Having Your Own Website

Building Quality Incoming Links To Your Site

Section III: Step-by-Step Checklist To Affiliate Success

Get organized and committed to the journey

Sign up for Pay Per Click programs

Sign up for Clickbank

Video Training

Article Marketing

Top 25 Article Directories

Build Squidoo Lenses and Hubpages

Autoresponders

Sign Up For Web 2.0 Social Networking Sites

Consider Building A Store

Set Up A Blog on a Free Site

Consider Setting Up Your Own Website

Getting Traffic To Your Site

INTRODUCTION

When it comes to going into business online, one of the easiest and most lucrative methods is through Affiliate Marketing. This is because becoming an affiliate marketer requires no experience, no website and simple promotional techniques that will convert prospective buyers into customers.

For the relative newcomer, affiliate marketing offers a planned method and blueprint to begin making sales online. There are a multitude of different opportunities, niches and markets to choose from. A person can become an affiliate for just about anything from digital products to flowers and everything in between.

In this book, we will cover the basics of affiliate marketing to give you an idea of where to start, how to get started and what websites are good to work with.

We will then move into how to become a profitable affiliate in 60 days or less, becoming an affiliate insider and some advanced techniques that if applied properly will take your earnings to the next level.

This book is not the end all in affiliate learning; instead, it is a good step-off point that will lead you to other books that will expand your horizons and earnings.

By the time you finish reading this book, you will be able to implement a concrete plan that will get you into earning money quickly and easily. These techniques have worked for a long time, and they work consistently to earn money from affiliate marketing if followed.

If you are already familiar with affiliate marketing, this book will give you new techniques to add to your marketing arsenal so that you can increase your affiliate earnings and expand on the methods that you use in order to be successful.

So, without further ado, let's get started on our journey to affiliate profitability!

Section I - What Is An Affiliate?

Basics of Affiliate Marketing

The concept of affiliate marketing is a variation on the outside sales position except that it all happens in cyber-space, and there is no door-to-door component. Think of yourself as the salesman, one of many, for a specific product or service and you've mastered the basics of what is an affiliate.

People have all kinds of products and services that they want to sell online.

Part of the process to become successful is to have a large amount of traffic that is interested in what you have to offer. The way you can accomplish this is by having salesman or affiliate promote your products. When a sale is made, you share the earnings with your affiliate/salesman through commissions.

Successful affiliates make a good living by promoting products and services of other vendors in order to make that commission.

For the purposes of this book, I will focus on one of the easiest affiliate networks to get started – Clickbank and list the others with a brief look at the larger networks. Once you learn how an affiliate network like Clickbank works, you will be able to expand that to other larger networks that have a myriad of different products and services that are commissionable.

Clickbank is one of the largest, oldest affiliate networks out there online. Clickbank sells only digital products, is extremely easy to learn how to use and has a ton of vendors just waiting to snap up a good affiliate.

There is no waiting time to become a part of the Clickbank affiliate family, and the commissions are much higher than the other networks, with some commissions going as high as 75%.

Clickbank is an affiliate network in that it is a whole bunch of vendors and affiliates all working under the umbrella organization called Clickbank. Through Clickbank, products and services are bought and sold, accounting goes on within the network and commissions are calculated per product sold. Before we go any further, let's look at what you can potentially earn from one product.

For example: You promote and sell on Clickbank product called Make Money Online: Get Paid For Life!. It sounds like a pretty exciting product, right? Well, it has the highest payout of any Top 10 Clickbank Product and is the Top Converting product offer online. It pays out at a 50% commission level.

When you look at it's pitch page, it is endorsed by some pretty heavy weight people including CNBC, As Seen On TV, Small Business Opportunities, Fox News, CBS News and Readers Digest.

As an affiliate, you will earn 50% of the $97 dollar price tag, and it's repaid on a monthly basis. So, that means that for every person who signs up through your affiliate link (which we will get in a minute), you will be paid $44 each month as long as that person stays signed up.

What do you think if you simply stuck with this affiliate program and reached their magical 100 referral mark. That's $4400 per month for promoting only one product.

Are you beginning to see how lucrative affiliate marketing can be?

Think about how much you could make if you found 10 affiliate programs like this one?

This is not only possible, but not that hard to accomplish if you know how.

Look on Clickbank and find 10 things that you think you might want to sell.

Make a list because as you learn more, you may want to revise it, and you may find that your choices are golden.

Affiliate Marketing 101 – The Basics

Since you are reading this book, I will assume that you are interested in making your fortune. Before you can even contemplate picking an affiliate program to join, you will need to make some basic changes in your thinking.

Change the way you think about money.

You've got to really change the way you view money and you want to begin to feel like you deserve to be wealthy. While this concept seems simple, many people don't feel like they deserve money.

As a result, their activities reflect their feelings of lack of worthiness. Instead of coming home from work and hitting the computer, reading an book, taking action on a plan, they will instead come home, sit in front of the television and time will pass.

Instead of becoming a veteran internet marketer, they will become the master of television watching.

People who feel like they should be able to make lots of money online will naturally make a lot of money online. This is not some spiritual mish-mosh, although I feel that spirituality is a part of everyone's journey. However, that is not what I'm talking about when I say people can make lots of money.

The most important thing to remember is that if you feel like you deserve lots of money, you will take the actions to make it happen.

It takes some basic things to be successful at affiliate marketing:

- Stay focused

- Pick a niche product to start with and then START

- Read this book and then take action.

- Make a schedule and then stick to it.

Start small and learn.

Avoid being overwhelmed out of the gate. You want to learn, apply it on a small level and then scale up when you feel you have the basics under control.

While you are doing this, you will start to make money. By staying focused, I mean avoid the multi-tab distractions. You can open a ton of websites in browser's nowadays. If your plan calls for answering email between a certain time and certain time, avoid reading emails before that time. Tell yourself, it will still be sitting there waiting for you at.

Research is key.

Clickbank

Clickbank has been in business since 1998, and has built their network to one of the largest retailer of digital products. With over 10,000 digital products, it is one of the premier affiliate networks. It is easy to use, easy to join and there are products in a ton of different areas from pets to electronics.

In order to earn commissions, all you need to do is take your affiliate ID and you get a link which you can use to send customers to. When they click on your link, it will record your commissions when they buy the product.

These affiliate networks generally require that you have a website that is related to the affiliate program you want to sell.

However, that's not impossible to accomplish, and you can get one at **www.blogger.com**, **www.typepad.com**, **www.wordpress.com** and the like. You can also sign up with very reasonable hosting services that provide one click installation of your blog site where you can start posting articles and blog posts related to the product or service you apply for at one of the larger networks like the ones listed below:

Clickbank is a Fast Start, Needs no website and pretty easy to be accepted into this program.

- **www.clickbank.com**

Need to have a website, makes sure that it's established with an About Us, Contact Us and Privacy page on the site. Should have a few weeks of posts at the very least.

- **www.shareasale.com**
- **www.cj.com**
- **www.rakutenadvertising.com**
- **www.amazon.com**
- **www.pepperjamnetwork.com**
- **www.datafeedr.com**
- **www.rubiconproject.com**

Wait at least 90 days before putting AdSense on your site. To ensure that you will be accepted to the AdSense program, it's best not to apply until you have an established site to show them.

- **www.adsense.com**

This serve is secondary and shouldn't be considered until you've got your sites up and running for a few months.

- **www.cpaempire.com**

Before you apply to any of the other sites, you need to have a real site. You will want to blog on the site for at least two weeks, one blog post per day.

If you aren't a writer, you will need to hire a freelancer. Go to **www.upwork.com**, **www.freelancer.com**, **www.fiverr.com** and the like to find a writer. You can hire a freelancer fairly inexpensively who will deliver you blog posts to add to your site.

Researching Your Products

Pick a niche product and start to research if it's a viable topic or subject. Whether you want to go with Clickbank products or with other affiliate products, you will need to do your research.

Finding a profitable niche should be your first type of research.

You want to have a product that is Hot! If you find a product that isn't very hot, don't expect to make any kind of money with it.

The reason I picked the Make Money Online is because it is a hot item. People are interested in the niche, and it's marketed well, presented in a professional manner, and has tools for its affiliates to use to make money.

To find out what are people looking to buy:

- Amazon Bestsellers: **www.Amazon.com**

- eBay Pulse: **www.Marketplacepulse.com/ebay/top-ebay-sellers**

- eBay Tera peak: Terapeak.com

Amazon.com Bestsellers

Amazon gives you a quick and easy way to find out what's hot and what's not on their site. It is a clear indicator of what the buying market is looking for, making it very easy for your to put yourself in the path of oncoming web traffic and make sales.

If you sign up with Amazon's affiliate program, you can sell all of the products on the site, and with the Bestsellers section, you will know for sure that certain products are selling. They even give you a Top10 list for each category so that you can use that to make articles, reviews and blog posts.

eBay Pulse Tool

This is a great place to find out what the hot products are because if a person is typing it into eBay, they are typing it into Google and Amazon. eBay Pulse gives you a real-time look at what people are looking to buy.

You can log into eBay and do a search on the completed items. It will tell you what people are selling, how many have sold and the average price. Look for items with bids, and this is a great way to get an idea of what people are looking for.

Terapeak is another great way to do things

Go to Hot Research, sort of like eBay pulse. It will give you a listing of what's hot on eBay. You can then drill down and it will give you an idea of some of the different auctions that are going on. If there are bids, this is a good item to become an affiliate for.

Hot Research > Hot Searches and then Search

Good average price above $30.00, with a good commission rate of no less than 40%, the higher the better. Also, don't go for the very high end products that are priced at above $125 dollars.

Section II – Newbie to Profitable Affiliate

Build Up To About 10 Products To Promote

As an affiliate, you will want to build up to about 10 products, so that you can mix up the top performing products and add the latest releases. While you should like what you're selling, don't be wed to it.

What may be a hot seller, may cool off and if you follow trends, you need to be able to move on. You don't want to add all these products at once, and build slowly as you get more experienced.

Because you don't want to overwhelm yourself with products, pick your products carefully. Choose popular products because you want to have top performing products.

Here are some things to remember when you are selecting products.

When you search for new products to promote from Clickbank, there are certain things that you are looking for.

First and easiest is the selection of the category that you want to work with. For instance, each affiliate products has some information that will help you make a good decision.

The three sites you will want to use to ascertain if a product is a good seller and a possible product you will want to promote includes:

- ➢ Clickbank Marketplace – **www.clickbank.com**

- ➢ CB Trends – **www.cbtrends.com**

- ➢ CB Engine – **www.cbengine.com**

Clickbank Marketplace

1. Sale Price: ($/Sale) This is the amount that affiliates are earning for referring customers. The amount earned is kept by Clickbank accounting and pays out every two weeks to the affiliate.

2. Percentage of Sale: (%/Sale) This is the average percentage commissions earned per affiliate per sale.

3. Referral %: This is the percentage of sales that people you refer

4. Gravity of Product: The gravity number is important because it shows the popularity of the product over time. Every time the product is sold or a new affiliate joins and uses the link the gravity of the program will change.

CB Trends

The popularity, price and commission paid of the product is very important.

When it comes to popularity or gravity, unless you are already a Super Affiliate avoid the products with very high gravity (125+), because it means that the market will be highly competitive and the chances of you making sales will be decreased accordingly. This applies only to Clickbank and not the other commission driven organizations.

In order to find out if a product is good to add to your affiliate arsenal, you will want to check it out at CB Trends (www.cbtrends.com) which is a free service that shows visual representation of what is on the Clickbank marketplace site making it easier to understand. There are some useful tracking tools that give you an easy way to see what is happening with the products you choose including:

➢ Popularity of the product

➢ Earning per sale

➢ Percent per sale

➢ Gravity

➢ Referrals

➢ Commission

If you take the visual representation, combine it with what you see on Clickbank's Marketplace, you will have a good idea of whether the product you're thinking about promoting is a good one.

Out of the 10 products that you pick to promote over time, you will want at least 6 of them to be popular. You want to mix it up so that at least half of what you're promoting is more competitive. The rest of the products should be up and comers, those products that are newer and building in the Marketplace.

CB Engine

CB engine shows you the new products and is an excellent tool to use if you want to focus on the new product releases. If you are going to work with Clickbank, which is a good first step into the affiliate arena, CB Engine should be one of the sites you bookmark and use.

It has a Brand New Products list, re-listed products with a ton of information to help you make an informed choice about the products you want to promote. Each product, new and re-listed, have graphs and visual representations about the health and viability of the products.

There are a couple of ways to go about finding out more about the product or service you are about to promote. First, you can buy the product.

Whether it's digital or tangible, buying and experiencing the product will usually make you a better promoter. However, with 10 products, that can become a bit pricey, so you may want to buy a couple products that you can afford, and look over the sales pages only of the remainder.

When looking over the sales or pitch page, you will want to think in terms of being a prospective buyer. Ask yourself some basic questions:

> Does the page, headline and opening paragraph grab your attention.

> Is the page easy to read in terms of colors, graphics and layout of the site.

> Is the message being presented clear and concise and easy-to-understand.

> Are there highlights of important facts, headlines to break up content and pictures that are relevant to the topic matter?

> Does the page lead you to the logical conclusion where you want to buy the product?

All of these things are important and will make or break you when people come through your referral link. Having a page where you want to buy the product will generally translate to high sales conversions. In that way, the traffic you drive to the product site stand a higher chance of buying in the end. If the page left you with a ho-hum, whatever feeling, it is probably quite possible that visitors arriving at the site will have the same reaction. As you go about promoting your affiliate products, make sure that you keep track of the products that are converting well, and the ones that are not. When you have a hot product that goes warm and then cold, you need to be ready to get rid of it. Earlier I told you not to get attached to a product or service. This is why. You have to know when to get rid of it.

Look at the choices you first made on Clickbank and ask yourself the questions from above. Are there any products that you might want to get rid of now?

Getting Traffic To Your Site

Video Promotion

While most people will tell you to use pay-per-click advertising, article marketing and building a website, here's a shortcut method to get your started and quickly. Videos can get you into search engines fast.

Use one of these tools to get started:

- Camtasia Studio has a 30 day free trial

- CamStudio which is free and located at http://camstudio.org

- Jing that works on the Mac or PC

- Web Cam

- Sony Movie Studio

- Movie Studio 9

Now that you have a selection of products, a website or direct links to a vendor's website, it's time to promote. First, you will want to get into the video arena.

I know you probably weren't expecting that. But, people are video junkies, and if you want to get people engaged, you will need to go where the traffic goes.

Creating videos is one sure-fire way to get traffic to your site. Creating a video is not as hard as you think. It's easy and fun, and will get you into the

---

Working with Camtasia can be a little daunting, but it will pay for itself in spades if you take the time to learn how to use it.

If you need to go free Jing is the second easiest way to record from screen to video. If you're good with PowerPoint, you can create a slide show, narrate it about your site and simply read from a script. These are the easiest type of video to create, and when used correctly, they are traffic bringers.

Set your monitor resolution to 800x600 for recording. Record your videos at 800 x 600, resized to 480 x 360 with Smart Focus. You want them to be quick, and talk about the product you are promoting.

The bottom third is very important in videos. You want to tell them about your domain name or the domain of the affiliate site. If you don't have a site of your own, go to Snip-URL where you can put in your affiliate link, and it will give you an output.

For instance, if your affiliate product is for Make Money Online, and your affiliate link is **http://XXXXX.PUBLISHER.hop.clickbank.net**, your Snip-URL will be: *www.snipurl.com/makemoneyonline*

The Snip-URL can go in the lower left part of your video, and remain there for the duration. As you talk about your website, all you need to do is use SnagIt to capture pictures, which you put in your PowerPoint presentation and capture as video.

Add a couple of transitions, and you are in the video arena. These short video reviews are what you upload to all of the video sites.

Things to remember:

➤ Make sure that the name of the video is your longtail key phrase or product name plus a word like deals. (ie. Salmon deals, Rolex watch deals)

➤ Make sure that the keywords and key phrases are submitted and enclosed in quotes as well as without quotes.

➤ Make sure that you submit them with the URL leading back to your website

➤ In the information section, be sure and put your website, or Snip-URL if you don't have a website that leads back to the affiliate product.

Pay-Per-Click Advertising

If you don't have a website, landing page or place to send prospective traffic, pay per click or PPC advertising is an excellent method to drive sales via your affiliate link.

Again, you will want to use discretion so that you don't wind up losing more money than you gain in sales. The largest PPC outfit is Google. Those little advertisements that you see on people's websites, plus on the side of the search results are called PPC advertising.

Advertisers pay a set amount per click in order to appear on sites. It is considered contextual advertising, because the advertising is related to the information being presented either in the search results or on the website. For instance, you won't get an advertisement for ice cream on a site about auto parts.

Adwords & Contextual Advertising

Advertising with Google is easy and deceptive to newcomers. Easy, in the fact that it is very easy to use; deceptive because if you aren't very careful you could lose a lot of money trying to get advertising that makes you money. Here are some techniques so that you can use the Adwords system and make money.

The site is located at: **http://adwords.google.com**

You can sign up for an Adwords account by clicking the Start Now button and filling in your information. Sign up for a standard and not a starter account. Adwords is pretty easy to use. Many people will want to start out with 100s of keywords and will take everything suggested by Adwords keyword tool.

Avoid this method and stick with a few terms that are laser-focused on your product or service.

Use the Adwords keyword suggestion tool or other keyword tool like Microinches Finder, Nichebot and Keyword Elite to find about five or six terms that are tightly related to your product.

You will want these keywords/key phrases to be low competition, high traffic words. The software just mentioned are designed to find keywords like this for your product.

You will want to drill down on your keywords. For instance, if your product is about dog health, don't just look at the keywords "dog health" and dogs. Look for things like "relief for dogs from fleas", "best dog food" or go into a specific breed like "cocker spaniel health", or "best dog food for beagles".

While you will get fewer visitors based on these keywords, the ones that will arrive will be very interested in your product. When you look at products, you will want to take this into consideration as well.

List your key phrases and base your advertisement around these key phrases. You will ideally want to get them into the title of your advertisement as well as in the listing for Adwords to use when listing when your ad will appear in the search results and on people's websites.

Use the Adwords keyword suggestion tool here:

https://ads.google.com/home/

Select key phrases that are relevant but not very competitive. Remember, that although you may only get 100 visits a day from a keyword, conversion rates are 1-2%, so that will usually equal a sale.

This is why you don't want to promote a product that is much cheaper than $30. If your commission is 50% to 75% of $30, that is $15.00 to $22.50 on each sale.

It has been shown that affiliates will convert on average 1% to 2% per 100 visitors if they have done adequate keyword/key phrase research.

It will generally convert the same on a $30+ item as it does on a $15.00 product. The amount of money you earn will only change due to the commission level and price of product.

Ad Variations

When you have your keywords in hand, go to Google and search on those keywords. Put the keywords between quotation marks and watch what comes up on the right hand side. This will give you great ideas on how to word your own advertisement.

Look at what ad is in the top spot 3 spots. Look at the titles they are using and see how you can word your advertisement similarly so that you get good clickthroughs. Then when you put together your initial ad, make some variations and track how many clicks each ad is getting. Keep the ad that performs the best.

When you are just starting out with Adwords, keep your bids low. Bid as little as $0.05 cents per click where you can, and just make sure that you get on page one of the search results.

Look towards doing advertising on websites only and forego the search results, because it is counted in 1000 impressions at a price and your money can go a longer way.

URL Display and URL Actual

One nice thing to remember is that you can put your Clickbank ID and URL in the Destination URL section of the advertisement. In the Display URL, you place the actual website URL of the affiliate products vendor.

Example:

Display URL: www.makemoney.com

Destination URL:

http://xxxxxx.makemoney.hop.clickbank.net/**?tid=MAKEMONEY**

That word "?tid=MAKEMONEY" on the end of the Clickbank ID is called a traffic tracking device which allows you to track how your campaigns are going. Both Clickbank and Adwords will allow you to track your advertising campaigns so that you can make a decision about what's working and what needs to be changed.

To track within Adwords, you will need to choose a keyword that you want to track in Adwords. Click on Edit Keyword Settings. Then you have a URL that you can add a tracking ID to which in this case would be "?tid=MakMoAd1" for MAKEMONEY, Ad #1. You only have 8 letters that you can use, so whatever you decide, it should be easy to understand and decipher.

Yahoo and MSN's Adwords Equivalent Contextual Advertising

While not much is said about the contextual advertising that is available through Yahoo and MSN, it does exist. As an alternative, you might want to consider advertising through them. The same rules apply, the competition is less and you may wind up spending a lot less for the same amount of advertising.

In order to figure out if it's worth the money, you can sign up for accounts with both MSN and Yahoo pretty easily and try it out. They also run a lot of specials and give away coupons worth various amounts of money just to get you to try their service.

Yahoo PPC Service: **https://smallbusiness.yahoo.com**

Microsoft Ads: **https://ads.microsoft.com**

While these are lesser advertised, contextual advertising outlets, you can get a lot of mileage from them, and all kinds of traffic you might have missed if you focused on Google alone. Remember, being successful as an affiliate means thinking outside of the box.

Facebook and Myspace Advertising

Often overlooked and very good places to advertise are Facebook and Myspace. While I wouldn't advertise the How To Make Money Online books, they are great places to advertise other digital products.

If, for instance, one of your products is Jamorama from Clickbank, it is a "learn to play guitar online" service that is made for young people, is done totally online and would make a great Myspace advertisement.

Squidoo and Hubpages

If you don't have a website and you want to have an intermediary page that gives more information and pre-sells the product more, you can use either Squidoo or Hubpages. They are free to build, takes about 60 seconds and requires no HTML ability to use.

Tons of people build Squidoo lenses using articles that expand on the products and services that they are promoting.

In this way, a person doesn't click through your link straight to the pitch page of the vendor and only think that you are trying to sell them something.

Through the use of these intermediary sites, you can add value to the product or service with a personalized set of information that is tailored to make the product more understandable.

If you decide to build a Squidoo page for your affiliate product, most people will do a review of the product or write an article outlining the benefits of using/reading/listening to the product. In this way, it is more personal and less salesman-like.

Web 2.0 Social Networking

By using Web 2.0 social networking, you can announce and spread the word about your affiliate product. Instead of sending them directly to the vendor's site, you can use Squidoo, Hubpages and other social networking sites like Ning and Scribd.com to Presell the product through writing articles and converting them into mini websites.

Instead of advertising the vendor site, you will advertise your intermediary site and use it to list build and follow up through an autoresponder.

The easy way to list build is take a picture of one of the aWeber or GetResponse forms using a program like Snagit, and upload the picture and make it a clickable link to a squeeze page. You can build a squeeze page using Weebly.com which has a drag and drop interface that makes it extremely easy to build web pages with autoresponder forms embedded in them.

You then have people click, go to your landing or squeeze page and fill out the form. On the landing page, you can further outline the benefits of the product you are promoting.

The Advantages of Having Your Own Site

While a lot of affiliate marketers can operate without setting up a website, the benefits of doing so will become immediately apparent. First, having your own website establishes your credibility on the subject, and further lends authority to the product you are promoting.

While you can strictly use Adwords and other contextual advertising methods, having your own website is a way to add other income streams, organize and consolidate your affiliate product offerings and add other types of advertising and monetization schemes to your site.

Setting up a website is not that difficult nor is it very expensive any more. If you decide to go with your own website, there are a few things you should know in order to get started. Get your own domain name. A domain name is a unique name that identifies your website. It transforms an IP address (100.99.103.44) to something memorable – www.yourdomain.com

Having your own domain name adds to the authority of what you're writing, should be easy to remember and gives you a platform from which to write. Registering a domain name nowadays costs only about $8 to $10. Some of the best registrars include:

➢ Ifastnet.com

➢ Godaddy.com

- ➢ Namecheap.com

- ➢ Internic.com

Next, you will want to get webhosting. This is also very inexpensive. A full featured webhosting plan will cost you only about $5.00 to $10.00 per month.

- ➢ Ifastnet.com

- ➢ Godaddy.com

- ➢ Hostgator.com

- ➢ Dreamhost.com

Get an easy to use website platform. You don't need to be an HTML or Dreamweaver expert to set up a really nice site.

The platform of choice these days is Wordpress, which is very simple to setup by using Fantastico and Cpanel, and there are tons of very nice themes out there for you to use. Two other easy to use content systems are Drupal and Joomla. All three of these will build out a full site for you that has an admin interface that is easy to learn and use.

Through the use of one of these platforms, you can accomplish a number of essential things to the success of your affiliate sales:

Affiliate link cloaking: It would be nice to think that everybody is honest. However, this is not the case. As a result, you need to cloak your affiliate link so that when a person clicks through your link and buys the product, the commission goes to you.

Especially with an affiliate network like Clickbank, it is very important to cloak your original link with an ironclad decoy link that keeps the commission protected.

It will take a link that looks like a mish-mash of letters and dots and like this: **http://AFFILIATE.PUBLISHER.hop.clickbank.net** and turn it into something like this: http://yourdomain.com/product.html. It makes it both easier to read and keeps your affiliate information secret and intact.

Pre-selling: This affords you the opportunity to write or have written articles that are keyword optimized (which means that they are designed to rank highly in the search engines for specific words), traffic magnets that affords visitors the opportunity to learn more about a specific product and get more exposure that leads to eventual conversion. Pre-selling is an art that happens over time.

Ad Tracking & Analytics: While Google Adwords offers excellent ad tracking features, having a person visit your website further refines the analytics you can look at.

As a visitor explores your entire website, you are gaining valuable information about what pages they visited how long they stayed on specific pages, what links they clicked and the like. All of this information can help you refine what is on your website.

For instance, say a person arrives at your home page, goes to a page on a specific product and then goes through a link on that page to another page on your site and stays there for a long time.

If this happens over and over, you have just gained valuable information about what has caught people's interest. In that way, you can offer more of the same that is on the second page so that people are likely to return and be re-exposed to you, your products and your site.

Blogging About Specific Topics Related To Your Affiliate Product: With a website built on the Wordpress platform, you can set up certain programs called plug-ins that automatically optimize your website. What this means is that Google and the other search engine spiders will love to stop by your site and add pages to their search index.

As you get more pages into the search engines, you will rank higher. What this means is that you will have more and more visibility and in turn more traffic will visit your site over time.

Learning about keyword research and search engine optimization or SEO is one of the things that every affiliate should learn. The more you know, the better your site will become, and the better your site, the more sales you will make.

Building Quality Incoming Links To Your Site

While you don't want to go link crazy, you will want to get a number of good incoming links from High PR link sites. Be careful – don't purchase links. While you can purchase links, it's frowned upon.

Step-by-Step Checklist To Affiliate Success

With everything you've learned to date, I'll bet your head is swimming. Below is a plan that you can implement to get you started on the road to affiliate success and profit.

Get Organized!

> Pick on affiliate network (I suggest Clickbank because it's easy). Spend a couple of hours learning the ins and outs of how it works. Look at the gravity, sale percentages and pick some products and make some affiliate links so that you are fully familiar with how the process works.

> Go to CB Trends and CB Engine and make sure you understand how they can help you pick winners.

> Stop by the Google Adwords tool and search for about 10 keywords for each product that you pick making sure that they are low competition, good traffic keywords and key phrases.

Keep good notes about what you are doing so that you can refer back to them later.

Sign up for Pay Per Click programs

Get yourself the following Pay Per Click accounts:

> ➤ Adwords, Yahoo Publisher and MSN AdCenter accounts

> ➤ Make a decision about whether you are going to build a website or work strictly through Pay Per Click advertising.

Sign up for Clickbank

> ➤ Sign up for Clickbank and get your nickname if you didn't do that yesterday.

Go through the help files at Clickbank, Adwords, etc. so that you understand basically how each program works.

Video Training

> ➤ Make a decision about which program you want to use to make your 1 minute videos.

> ➤ Look on YouTube and search under Camtasia training. You will find a ton of videos on how to make a decent video.

- ➢ Check out **https://advertising.adobe.com** for free uploading of your videos after they're done. If you want more options, there is a paid portion that will allow you to submit to more video sites. Also, you can consider Traffic Geyser for maximum coverage with videos, if you have some money to spend. **www.trafficgeyser.com**

Article Marketing

Article Marketing is one of the easiest ways to get steady traffic to your website. Using good keyword/key phrase research will get you a ton of traffic as you write articles based on the results. In those article directories, you can put links back to your site and that will send traffic your way.

- ➢ Never submit the same article to multiple sites

- ➢ You need to change your article by at least 50% for each site. This is not as hard as you might think. Check out Unique Article Wizard located at: **www.uniquearticlewizard.com** on how to accomplish that.

Top 16 Article Directories

1. **ezinearticles.com**

2. **articlesBase.com**

3. **buzzle.com**

4. **pubs.acs.org**

5. **goarticles.com**

6. **articlealley.com**

7. **articledashboard.com**

8. **articlesnatch.com**

9. **ideamarketers.com**

10. **webpronews.com**

11. **amazines.com**

12. **upublish.info**

13. **isnare.com**

14. **articlesfactory.com**

15. **web-source.net**

16. **articleblotter.com**

Build Squidoo Lenses and Hubpages

➢ Get some free pages which can act as intermediary sites which you can use to pre-sell your various products by writing articles presenting the products and writing about the features and benefits.

➢ Build one Squidoo or Hubpages per article and product. Avoid combining stuff on pages, because you want to give a clear message about each product or service that you are promoting.

- You can build more than one page per product. Look and think about the different angles you can bring to each product or service that you are promoting.

- For instance: list the features and benefits in general lens, then build 4 or 5 lenses on specific sub-features where you only talk about that feature. Then, from the main lens or Hubpages, you can link to the sub-feature pages.

Autoresponders

Autoresponders are e-mail messages that are sent automatically when an e-mail arrives for a specific e-mail account. The most common example of an autoresponder is the ubiquitous "Out of Office" message sent by mail programs like Outlook and Eudora.

Web autoresponders are used by affiliate marketers to send responses to questions when they are away from the computer.

Autoresponders will answer questions, send information about a product or service. They are also key to list building which is where many affiliate marketers make backend sales by sending follow-up messages. Most web autoresponders give you unlimited auto response messages, and you can have multiple autoresponder addresses.

Autoresponders are inexpensive and are considered your silent 24/7 salesman. Two good autoresponder companies that charge around $20 bucks a month include:

- AWeber – **www.aweber.com**

- GetResponse – **www.getresponse.com**

There are many other autoresponder companies out there, and you can even get autoresponders as part of your webhosting package.

However, these two autoresponder companies offer a host of addition features and benefits that allow you to build a list super-fast.

Backend sales on follow-up messages accounts for a large part of affiliate sales. It is a known fact that people need multiple exposures to a product to convert tire-kicking to sales.

Sign Up For Web 2.0 Social Networking

It is very important to sign up for as many Web 2.0 social networking sites so that you can promote your product pages – whether they're on Squidoo, Hubpages or Weebly. In this way, you can build a steady flow of traffic to your pre-sales pages, build your list with an autoresponder form and increase sales.

The Top Sites To Sign Up For Include:

> Digg – **www.digg.com** - Digg is a website made for people to discover and share content from anywhere on the Internet, by submitting links and stories, and voting and commenting on submitted links and stories, in a social and democratic spirit. Propeller – **www.propeller.com**

> News vine – **www.newsvine.com** – News vine allows you to report on the news that you find around the net. If you have a website, News vine is a great way to get the news out about it. News vine also allows you to create your own blog, so you write articles, post reviews about products and more just like you have your own site.

> StumbleUpon – **www.stumbleupon.com** - Boasting 2.5 million users, StumbleUpon is a web browser plugin that allows its users to discover and rate web pages, photos, videos, and news articles

> LinkedIn - **www.linkedin.com** - 575 million members - a powerful tool for business networking.

> Orkut - **Orkut.com** is an Internet social networking service run by Google Now has a membership of 57 million.

> Twitter – **Twitter.com** is a free social networking service that allows users to send "updates" (text-based posts that are up to 140 characters long) via SMS, instant messaging, email, the Twitter website, or an application such as Twit terrific.

- Yahoo! 360 (a.k.a Yahoo! Days) is a personal communication portal similar to Orkut and Myspace -- it is currently in the beta-testing phase. It integrates features of social networking, blogging and photo sharing sites.

- Xanga – **xanga.com** with 40 million members. Xanga is a free Web-based service that hosts weblogs, photoblogs, videoblogs, audio blogs, and social networking profiles.

- Ryze – **ryze.com** with 25 million members. Ryze.com is a free social networking website designed to link business professionals.

Consider Building A Store

As an affiliate, you can build a store or join a program where a store is provided for you. There are a number of Clickbank-ready stores that are pre-set up. You only need to pay a onetime fee and the store will be activated in your name with your affiliate ID. So, instead of promoting just 10 products, you can promote the entire Clickbank host of vendors. There are ups and downs to this.

Pros: All the work is done for you. There is a Featured section to these stores where you can highlight the 10 products that you are actively promoting. It also gives you a quick web presence and if you don't have website building experience, everything is done for you.

Cons: Your store look just like every other person who bought the store package. Because it is built for you, it is a standardized template, so there can be hundreds, even thousands of other stores out there that are just like yours.

Set Up A Blog on a Free Site

Take a short bit of time to set up a blog on one of the free sites, or build a site and get webhosting. Whichever you decide, having a small site that is yours will go a long way towards building your credibility for the long term. Using PPC (pay per click) is fine up to a point. However, to expand and grow with products and services, having a site is essential.

Free Websites:

Wordpress: **www.wordpress.com** – You can get a blog started in less time than it takes you to read this sentence. All you need is an email address. You'll get your own WordPress.com address (like you.wordpress.com), a selection of great free and customizable designs for your blog (called themes) and 3 GIGABYTES of file storage.

There is a great deal of help and instruction to show you what to do and how to get started. Your website address would be something like https://product.wordpress.com and you can build as many of these free sites as you like. The positives of using the Wordpress.com system is that you are on a domain that has a very high page rank, lots of visitors and tons of help. Even if you've never set up a blog before, it's so easy that you can get started and not feel overwhelmed.

Blogger: Another free platform that is owned by Google is great to set up a blog on. Again, you will be a subdomain like http://product.blogspot.com, but it's free, there's no webhosting fees involved and you can set it up without any HTML, programming or web design experience. You simply pick from one of the many themes presented, and your blog is ready to go. Having a Blogger blog gets you listed in Google (since they own it), and makes it easy to get your message out there.

Joomla: Although Joomla is free, they don't have a free site where you can build on a subdomain. Joomla is an award-winning content management system (CMS), which enables you to build Web sites and powerful online applications.

Many aspects, including its ease-of-use and extensibility, have made Joomla the most popular Web site software available. Best of all, Joomla is an open source solution that is freely available to everyone.

With that said, Joomla has a ton of online help just like Wordpress; however, you will have to get webhosting and a domain name to use it.

Consider Setting Up Your Own Website

Whichever platform you decide on – Wordpress or Joomla – you will need webhosting, a domain name and it will take a bit of time to get things set up.

Most affiliate marketers tend to go with either Blogger or a Wordpress blog and self-hosting. Joomla is an option, but the learning curve is a little bit longer. So, if you're looking to get going, you might want to consider either the free services or Wordpress.

Once you decide on getting your own blog, select inexpensive webhosting. Remember, webhosting should have cPanel or One-Click setup attached to it. HostGator has cPanel and Fantastico and Dream host has One-Click. Both perform the same function – set up of Wordpress with no knowledge of MySQL, Wordpress or FTP.

This is the quickest way to get started with your blog. Once it's set up, you will need to look at article writing. If you're not a writer, check out the freelancers at Elance, Guru.com and Rent coder.

Getting Traffic To Your Site

Write down and plan the methods you are going to use to drive traffic to your website: Pay-Per-Click, Squidoo and Hubpages, article marketing, social networking and the like. Then schedule when you will be posting to your site, and posting to social networking sites.

In the end, if you follow this entire checklist and don't give up, you will begin to see sales for the products that you are promoting.

You can also add more products over time to promote, build more than one website, put up Squidoo and Hubpages highlighting your various products and services and add things like AdSense to further monetize your site.

HOW TO START A BLOG

Ever wondered how to start a blog and make enough money to quit your job?
With this book You can do it. Tons of people already have.
Start today you too.

(<u>BONUS 3</u>) – FREE BOOK - By : "Santiago Johnson Smith"

TABLE OF CONTENTS [BONUS 3 – FREE BOOK] - HOW TO START A BLOG

Blog Basics

A blog is sometimes called web log or weblog. At first, they were used as a personal place, for collecting links, sharing commentary – but now; they are a valid and VALUED form of communication for business people of all types. From the basics of blogging, to the intermediate areas – such as social bookmarking, and article marketing, to the advanced techniques using auto responders and more, there's something for every affiliate marketer to put into motion.

The great thing about blogs is that people read them for fun and for information – in fact, blogging is one of the few areas of the internet that covers business, pleasure, networking and play.

They do for your company what face to face marketing could only do in the past – they provide you with a real, interesting connection to your readers – personalised contact, and information about your company that will allow them to empathise, and discuss your most important points, and anything that ties in with hot button topics and your business.

Blogs give your readers and consumers a chance, not only to read and connect with you, but a chance to comment and discuss with you, and your team, the information that you're sharing – allowing them to further relate to your message. And a consumer that relates to you is a customer in waiting!

Our guide covers the very basics of blogging – it skims into areas that you'll possibly never have heard of – and cover them so that you can employ them in seven days – or less.

Step 1

Starting a blog is as simple as finding a space online to write – and the time to write.

To start though, you'll need to work through a brief list of steps to create your space.

Before you even consider your blog though, you have to think about WHAT you're going to blog about. It's important to stop and think about your blog, before starting it because, to be quite honest, without purpose, blogs are pointless. And this pointlessness will dilute your message considerably.

So, you need to think about what you're writing and why. Consider your theme – and then build some keywords around it, because for the first little while, you should try to include at least some of them in every post. You'll get archived in all of the right places that way, which will lead valuable NON COMMENT generated traffic to your blog. You'll also be commenting on blogs similar to yours and hopefully, generating more traffic based on the links you leave.

You can choose your topic, keyword, and theme simply by considering what, in connection to your business you're an expert in. Once you've looked at that, you can decide whether it's profitable, or viable to pursue it. If not, look at a related area that you can cover – your blog should always relate to your business choices, and give you interested traffic. Having said that, your blog isn't a free advertising system and nothing more – you've got to remember that people will be turned off by blatant advertising.

Choosing your keywords

Keyword Research

Keyword research is relatively simple – you can undertake basic research at

https://ads.google.com/home/tools/keyword-planner/

You can use this to research your general keywords – and check on their general profitability, if you're using CPM advertising. You might not be – but most blogs make a residual income from AdSense or similar, and it's not something you should overlook, for your long term stratagem. Niche blogs can earn well.

Once you've found a profitable overall keyword, you'll need to check out your competition :

https://www.wordtracker.com/

Though considered less effective now – it's still a good tool for finding your competition levels. You'll be able to assess your competition – basically, you're looking for a niche that's either tiny, if it's narrow, or large, if it's broader. Your narrower niches can only support a tiny amount of blogs – whereas the broader your definition, the more your niche will support – but the flip side to that, is that you've got more competition.

Once you've worked out your profitability, and competition, you can also use the keyword search at Overture to evaluate your other keywords (and get an idea on where to start blogging from).

You can place that information in a spreadsheet for reference – or use programs like article architect to extend on your research (affiliate link for article architect)

Once you've made a list of your keywords – and paced them into a spread sheet, you can take your research a step further. Article architect does it for you, but if you've not got that piece of software, or a similar one that researches keywords, you can do it manually.

Open up both Google and Yahoo, and start plugging your keywords into it – at the top you'll see a listing 1 of (a number) – you can then divide your 'competition' number by the total of your searches (a number) – that will give you a rating for that keyword – and the keyword with the 'best' ratings are the ones you'll probably want to focus on.

Article architect does this automatically – highlighting the 'optimum' keywords – and there are other pieces of software will do the same.
The reason you're doing this is to see where your keywords will have the best chance of ranking – you'll be able to find the best place to 'position yourself' this way.

Keep those keywords handy – you'll need them when you start writing content.

Got your keywords? What do you want to blog about?

Once you've got your keywords, you'll have an idea, at least, of the profitable areas of your niche that you can take advantage of. You'll be able to choose an interesting niche – for both you to write in, and your prospective readers.

You'll find that you can narrow it down pretty easily based on what you've got on your keyword lists – and what YOU feel like you want to write.

While its important to work out what you want to do with your blog, based on your view of profitability, it's also important to remember that working based on keywords alone is a sure fire way to build an impersonal, and possibly unmotivated blog for your readers.

Step 2

Look at what you're ABOUT to do from a reader's perspective

One of the more important actions anyone creating or 'cleaning up' a blog can do is look at what you're doing or about to do from the perspective of average Joe reader.

Average Joe doesn't care about profitability. He doesn't care that you're optimising to make the most out of PPC clicks. He REALLY doesn't care that you've worked hard in getting your information into the search engine – and in front of them.

ALL he cares about is what they are looking for – and they are hoping that YOUR site is the site that will provide it.

Average Joe will remain on your site and read ONE POST in for anywhere up to 30 seconds. They might then click on your PPC advertising – they might sign up for your newsletter – they might read more of your posts (yes!) or, if your site doesn't live up to what they were expecting – what they were looking for, they'll click away, either back to the search engine, or to their next option from the search engine.

Blogging isn't just about eyeballs on your page – it's about eyeballs on your page, and comments in your inbox. People have to have a reason to come back, and the simplest way to ensure that is to ensure you've got a reason for them to WANT to visit your site again.

This stickivity is what makes blogging so tantalising- if you can get it right, your blog will attract Average Joe, Average Jane and all of their friends, because the best blogs get commented on in other places – and shared with others.

So, from a reader's perspective is your blog going to fulfil a) your niche and b) give your readers quality, quantitative content that will either strike a controversial or empathic chord with them, giving them something to comment on.

Give Your Readers What They Want

Studies suggest that there's up to a quarter of the internet reads blogs – that's a lot of eyeballs. And on top of that, another study suggests that there's two blogs founded every minute. Two blogs a minute is 120 blogs an hour – and nearly 3000 a day. Take that to its logical conclusions and that's a lot of blogs competing for a less rapidly increasing source of traffic.

More than that though, blogs are competing for a specific NICHE of readers – though its true that some blogs will pull in readers from search engines, blogs still don't have the impact of static sites – and the average internet user may not know HOW to search blogs.

Once you've got the absolute best information in your niche, you can be sure that you'll attract the right kinds of traffic, and that they'll attract MORE traffic by referencing you on their sites – bookmarking you, and more.

Blogging is all about the reader – ultimately, its not about how well you position yourself, or how strongly you optimise your site – though you can bookmark yourself, and generate a certain amount of traffic that way – the best sites have faithful readers that bookmark and discuss the site independently of ANY input from the site owner (you).

The best blogs are one or a mix of tips and advice, hobby or interest discussion, technique and connection. When blogging, if you can make a connection with your reader, then you've won most of the battle. 'Connecting' with your readers is as simple as being personable, and approachable, and giving people a chance to empathise with you.

Who is your reader?

Thinking about what your reader wants to see lets you work out WHO your reader is. Which you'll need later too, to advertise your blog effectively.

So who IS your ideal reader?

Do they have a specific interest, within your niche?

ULTIMATELY, when you know who your reader is, you can plan the creation of a blog that will fully appeal to any readers you attract. If you've planned on whom you're targeting, you'll find it far easier to write content that will continue to satisfy your readers, whilst giving you room to evolve and plan more content as you grow.

Got all of that sorted out?

Now you can move onto the technical stuff!

Step 3

Choosing your platform

There are several major platforms to blog on, but for simplicity's sake, we're only going to focus on three options: Wordpress (self-hosted), Wordpress (hosted) and Blogger. All three give you strong, steady options to blog from, and all three are easy to configure – and best of all, all three should integrate with any structure you've already created or are planning to create within your business.

You may find, however, that you can't integrate the self-hosted Wordpress with your site, but you should find that you can find a complimentary template on most good self-hosted Wordpress blogs.

Wordpress – self hosted

By far and away, one of the most popular options for anyone that is serious about their blogging, the self-hosted Wordpress option. You can install your blog anywhere on your site, and its completely within your control, which means YOU can choose what you'd like to have running – an important feature if you're looking to add the ability to do things like email the information to people, or polls. Or your own advertising in some cases.

By far and away, the easiest way to install Wordpress is via Fantastico – most cPanel hosts offer both Fantastico and the ability to install up to date Wordpress. Otherwise, you can find instructions online at **https://wordpress.org**

You can choose your own themes, your own plugins – and modify it in any way you see fit.

Wordpress (hosted)

Hosted Wordpress is a secondary option for anyone whose hosting won't support the Wordpress self-install options. You can grab blogs from lots of places, but places like **https://wordpress.com** won't allow you to run a commercial blog.

Hosted Wordpress blogs will only ever offer the very basics of WordPress blogging – you can't control the themes on offer, which means you can't choose a specific theme – unless it's already installed on the site. The same applies to plugins.

Blogger

Blogger is a Google owned blogging system, and is highly popular with non tech savvy people. It gives you a basic frame to build on – and is less flexible than either version of Wordpress hosted blogs.

However, Blogger is a great option if you really don't want to modify anything to do with your blog, other than the theme and possibly add some surface widgets.

Blogger also lets you archive your blog on your own site, giving you all of the benefits of self-hosting with none of the update headaches.

Ultimately, there are more software options for your blog – such as Moveable Type (Perl based) and Type pad (hosted, by the same company that offers Moveable Type and LiveJournal). Moveable type is not free for commercial purposes – another one that isn't free, but is a really solid blogging package is Expression Engine – again, you'll have to make sure that you get a valid licence for it, for the purposes you want to use it for.

What about CMS's?

I'm not recommending any of the CMS based systems, despite the fact that you can use them to build really nice, really strong blogs; you can't use some of the nicer features of blogging that you really need to take full advantage of, to get the most out of your efforts.

Most CMS systems don't have tagging protocols, track backs and pinging - though they have ways to leave comments per article or post, you'll find that they are lacking for full featured blogs.

All of the options will give you a blog that you can build a solid base from, but of course ultimately, where you want to build your blog, be it on your own website or via Blogger (to archive on your site) or hosted with another site, you'll have to stick with what you choose – purely for the fact that you're going to be promoting it – and the last thing you want is to move on after a couple of weeks cause you've played with the others and discover you prefer one over the other.

There is NO HARM in testing them all out first and getting comfortable, if you've never blogged – or haven't explored for a while. Wordpress (self-hosted) is easy to install 'vanilla' (no plugins or themes) via Fantastico – just follow the instructions presented and it'll install a simple Wordpress install in around three clicks.

Once you've gotten comfortable you'll need to decide on your theme – you'll also want to pick plugins for Wordpress, play with certain features in Blogger, and add widgets in other programs. We'll cover the plugins and other features for Blogger at the end of the book – for the moment, all you need do, now, is to find a theme you're comfortable with.

Picking a theme

Most people that found blogs have great plans – they want to write interesting content (that makes them money for their effort) and they want to be THE site that people come to for their information.

Most people don't consider what they want their site to look like though. Whether this is a deliberate oversight or if they just don't know what to do with their theme, it's probably one of the biggest 'beginner' mistakes that anyone can make.

Blogger comes with lots of pre-installed themes – or you can add your own CSS to it, to give it your 'unique' look. Its important to at least personalise any theme you choose be it on Wordpress(self-hosted) or Blogger – its not possible on hosted versions of Wordpress, or at least, not as easily. There are customisable options on Wordpress.com but they cost money and they are still aren't as flexible as you can have on your own site, so aren't as customisable as you really need to present a professional image for yourself and your blog.

There are many themes that you can choose from – and it can kind of be like decorating your first house – lots of fun, but very wearing!

Wordpress:

https://wordpress.com/themes
https://nicepage.com/wordpress-themes
https://athemes.com/collections/free-wordpress-themes/
https://www.templatemonster.com/it/temi-wordpress-gratis/

All of the above sites allow you to use their themes for free, though its well worth checking the licences – some are completely open – others are restricted simply to personal use.

You can also buy templates from professional designers – or look around and see who other people are using. It's a fair bet that your colleagues or favourite blogs will have designers to recommend highly.

Blogger

Unsurprisingly most Blogger template sites are actually hosted ON Blogger, so you've got a vast array of free blog themes.

https://sites.google.com/view/free-blogger-templates/

https://colorlib.com/wp/free-blogger-templates/

https://btemplates.com/

The final site also contains a lot of wonderful tips out with the scope of this guide, about how to add more features, such as web albums and forms.

Themes are easiest described as the thing that 'skins' your site to look different – more than that though, your theme controls ALL of the appearance of your blog – it's not just the wall paper on the walls, but the walls themselves in some cases.

Step 4

Blog content

Putting the cart before the horse?

Writing for the web isn't a case of collecting your ideas and then putting them online – and blog posting especially is a hidden and deceptively simple looking 'art form' all of its own.

Before you actually write one word of content though you need to think about what you're going to say. You should have your keywords organised into some sort of coherent list – and you should be weeding out the ones you're not interested in using. Once you've done that, you need to sit down and plan down your blog. You need to plan at least 20 posts and choose some sort of posting schedule.

Once you've planned your content, you can start writing your posts. In the case of WordPress, you can queue your posts as you are writing them, giving you the additional advantage of being able to post series and have them ready to go, without losing your flow. If you're using blogger, you should still write your posts as you can then simply copy and paste them into your blog on the day you want them to go live.

We always recommend that you stay at least three posts ahead of your posting schedule – that way, if you hit a dry spot, or find yourself too busy to post; you've still got 'emergency' content on tap, till you can re-evaluate.

What should a blog post BE?

Blog posts should follow one of a few formulae, but before you look at them – you should probably consider what they can and can't contain – there are a couple of 'no no's' in blogging.

First and foremost – your blog should be advertising light, if it contains any advertising at all. People don't want to talk about your latest and greatest advert – they want to read about your opinions and thoughts in your niche – they want to know that you DO actually know what you're talking about, and most importantly, they want to discuss, not be sold to.

This means that though your blog will do the job of promoting your product, you have to do it without being blatantly, obviously advertorial.

You CAN write about products – talk about why you're so passionate about them – their features, the things that make you want to use them – or the services, or problems they solve.

You also don't need to just WRITE – you can upload pictures, podcasts (audio), video, multimedia – in fact, the more interactive your blog is, without intruding on the experience of the average visitor, the more traffic and return visitors you'll get and the more comments your blog will garner.

Writing for the web

Writing for the web is an art form.

You need to use short sentences, with subheadings, usually one per paragraph – those sub headings should be bolded, to stand out, because studies have proven, without a shadow of a doubt that the majority of internet users, especially those with a lower technical savvy than usual, skim read.

They skim read because we've been conditioned to believe two things about the internet: there's a lot of good information out there – but it can be incredibly hard to find, even on 'trusted' sites. Google's quality, page rank and duplicate content algorithms go a long way to helping to sift the dross from the perfect, but we're still left with people gaming the system, or worse, not being able to clearly state what we, ourselves are looking for.

Back to Average Joe for a minute. He doesn't know how to use Boolean operators, in fact, it sounds too complex maths like to be of any interest to him, and many internet users don't search for things as much as ask Google questions.

Keyword searching is a really good technique to learn, but for most people typing in short phrases, or whole questions, is the way to go, complete with punctuation.

Depending on the sophistication of the software in question, they might get exactly what they are looking for, but the same studies that suggest people skim read, also tell us that people really don't understand how to get the most from the internet.

It was best summed up in the X-files – the truth is out there – but where?

Skim reading users do have their advantages – internet writing doesn't need to be tight – just on one (tiny) topic. Blog posts can cover one tiny minutiae of a subject and then head back, stating it differently, another day.

There is one exception to this rule – when the situation or post doesn't warrant that style, don't use it. It's easy for someone to suggest that you blog using subheadings, but if you're blogging about yourself and your family, you might find it very hard.

Blogging is ultimately about YOUR BRAND and YOUR STYLE, so use it well, and you can't go wrong.

The most popular blog post formula

Blogging has fallen into several styles, like articles in newspapers and magazines. You can write and choose to use several different formulae, but ultimately, you have to find a way, and a style of writing that is comfortable for you.

The most common and most responsive way of blogging is 'problem – solution'. You take one common problem or current trend, or newsworthy topic and you 'solve' it.

Solving it can be as simple as providing your opinion, showing where you stand on any given issue, or it could be offering an actual solution to a problem many of us encounter.

Problem – solution or 'action – reaction' blogs are very popular with a vast majority of readers, but aren't without their inherent problems.

For a start, if you're 'solving' a current newsworthy item, although you are giving people a view of the fact that you are, in fact human, you'll also find that unless you are being very careful about expressing your views, you're going to upset someone, somewhere along the lines.

This can be a good thing – being of conviction in what you're saying not only gives you the authenticity that most blogs lack, for fear of stirring up trouble, but will also promote conversation – but not all of the conversation you promote will be positive.

You have to take the good with the bad and accept that no matter what you do, you'll always ruffle some feathers – just like in real life.

Another type of highly popular blog post is the review.

It's fairly straight forward to write a review post, but you've got to be careful. If it doesn't fit with the theme of your blog, you'll find that it actually damages your overall traffic. Your blog should always be laser focussed on the niche you want to talk about, and related areas to the niche. You can't go off topic!

Another type of post is 'a list' – lists of the ten most popular (x)'s.

(x) reasons why (y) is the only option/ a very bad idea

(x) reasons why you should/should not do (y)

(x) lifesaving hacks.

The highly popular blog, **https://lifehacker.com** is full of these tips and tricks – an article centred on solving a problem. The problem may not be implicitly stated, but instead touched on in general terms, but the solutions are always bang on the money, and that makes this blog a must read.

Its style is easy to emulate too. What problems does your niche have – are there several solutions (that you know of?) and can you express them in simple terms?

The final type of post that is very popular and easy to write is the feature – features can be one article, or several long articles, with links to each other. They should cover something important and be packed full of information. Keyword rich, you want your readers to come away feeling like they've really learned something, and search engines to come away with a whole new platter of wonderful content to add to their indexes.

The art of writing itself

Ultimately, you have to remember that though some blogs are founded for personal gain, if you're working on it to make any sort of income at all; you need to consider that your blog is a marketing project. You're either marketing the content, your company, or in some cases, yourself.

Once you've gotten your head round that, you'll also understand why you can't use slang, or make spelling or grammar mistakes, but more importantly, you'll realise that blogging might be the one 'voice' or face you present to people, so you'll need to offer a consistent, interesting brand.

There are specific, specialised types of post that work well with blogs from an internet marketer's point of view – like information about your company. Go beyond FAQ's and contact information – and share the nitty gritty about your operation. Make your blog readers feel like they are getting in on a secret of some description – or share something that wouldn't ordinarily be online – such as your motivation for going into business.

You can also recommend other marketers that you like, without appearing too fawning, if you're honest. Talking about experience is a sure fire way to improve on both your customer image, and your professional image.

You can also....

Use your blog to archive articles and other freebies for your company.

More importantly than that though, always ensure that you've got somewhere in your blog for people to sign up to your mailing list. Giving them the option to do that will also mean that you've got multiple traffic streaming to and from you blog, and though it seems odd to set up like this at first, people ARE more likely to sign up for your newsletter (with and without incentives!) if they like what you're saying on your blog.

As an extra bonus, you can 'tie' your blog feed to your auto responder, giving people the option of signing up to receive your posts by email – thus negating the need to come to your site until you post – we've covered that in the 'advanced' section of this book.

It has been suggested that there's a definite link between people that sign up for your newsletter, and people that comment on blogs attached to newsletters – and these people are the ones that are interested, interactive readers. They have a vested interest in commenting on your blog.

Style AND substance

Blogging isn't just about providing search engine content, and though its a great way to make connections with your customer base, the most important thing to remember is that shallow content breeds shallow contacts.

What this means is that if you're posting trivial stuff, people that are interested in little more than the trivial stuff will read your blog, and no one else.

Post about the 'meaty' stuff – and you're more likely to not only getting responses, but to gain responses that will help you further shape your content to fit your readers.

Though you will start out with a strong plan, and should try to stick to that as much as possible for the first few months (so as not to confuse yourself or waste the research you did in founding the blog) you should also consider the needs, wants and interests of your readers. Do THEY comment on more of one type of content? Can you write to fit the things they are raising?

Purely from a stylistic point of view, blogging works far better when you're using the active tense (Our newest division opened – we're putting the finishing touches to a launch) rather than the passive (our new division was opened – we've been working on a launch) – passive tense is both flat and doesn't contain energy. Its motionless, and doesn't give the impression of dynamism, which, when keeping a blog is very important.

Speaking of dynamic – ALWAYS be enthusiastic!

Blogging should never be a chore, and if it begins to feel that way, you really need to stop and question WHY.

Blogging is about sharing your passion, your enthusiasm, and your experience with others, and to do that, you've got to believe in what you're writing. If you don't, then how can you expect your readers to enjoy and comment?

If you love what you blog, you'll never work a day on your blog, in your life ;)

Step 5

Promoting Your Blog

Just putting your blog online is not enough. Once your content is off to that flying start (and its perfectly acceptable to found a blog and then backdate a couple (though, not too many!) posts to give your readers something to read. So over days 1 to four, you should have decided what to blog about, created and installed your blog, made sure you've got enough content to last you at least a month and posted it.
Now what?

Well, the long and short of it is, NOW comes the hard work – NOW you have to promote your blog.

Promoting your blog will put it in front of people. Fortunately, there's a myriad of ways to do it, but, unfortunately, they all take time.

Blog Marketing Ideas and concepts

You'll want to make sure that once your blog is developed and in place that its positioned perfectly to capture your market – in doing so you'll find that your blog markets itself.

To start with though, you've got to find your niche – the USP you want to target.

Defining your blog's USP is easy – what sort of reader do you want to attract, and what are they interested in? Does your blog cover it?
That's IT!

Once you've worked out your blog's USP, you can then plan where you want to advertise and approach readers – you'll also be able to track down competitors and colleagues in the arena that your blog. You'll need to know about them to know where best to comment!

Make Your Blog pull people in...

Your blog should, quite literally, mesmerise people and draw them in – interest them in reading about your opinions and information, and most of all, be completely on point for what they were expecting. Your blog should contain as much unique information as you can possibly manage, whether you've rewritten it from PLR or written your content from scratch – it should ALWAYS be unique. You'll avoid Google's duplicate content filter, and better than that, you'll get a reputation for not following the herd.

In the case of internet marketing, this does include ads about launches, but one of the biggest mistakes most bloggers (and mailing list owners!) are making is that they think that they HAVE to share the mailing information they've been given, as an affiliate.

This is a mistake because like seeing the same image over and over again, people will start to block out affiliate based ads – so instead of sharing what you've been given, verbatim, how about writing your own ads?

Its unique content and will interest people far more than flashy music or templates, but having said that, you do need to consider making your blog at least a little memorable. Choose a template that speaks to you on a professional level, but is uncluttered, unfussy, and most of all, interesting and easy to use. There's no point in using a flash template or a FLASHY template if you've got little to no clue how to make it work.

Making your customers aware your blog exists is a bit harder, but not impossible.

Most internet marketers have access to forums, mailing lists and more – so use them to tell people about your blog. If you're lucky, a 'big dog' marketer will see what you're talking about, and link to you – hint, talk about them, though don't say anything untrue! - and you'll probably get some spill over. These 'big dogs' might also consider running a solo ad for you, but you may have to pay for it, and unless you're in exactly same niche as them, or at least one that overlaps considerably, this may not be all that worthwhile for you.

More ways to let people know you exist.

Blogging is an emergent technology – you have to keep this in mind, because if its an emergent technology, so are the ways you promote your blog.

You can promote blogs via link exchanges designed specifically for blogs. There's several of them including:

https://blogcatalog.com
(in this case it only accepts blogs on the Wordpress platform)

Blog catalogues are probably a very good way to get a very small, but very targeted amount of traffic – usually around a similar level to submitting to places like

https://www.searchenginejournal.com/submit-your-site-to-yahoo-and-dmoz-directories/1440/

(a directory for everything online, edited by humans).

Blog link exchanges are less common, despite the fact that there's technology in place, on most every blog, to allow people to share important links, but so far, there's been very little in the way of 'automatic blogrolling' possibly because its so open to abuse.

There are sites though, that run link exchanges specifically for blogs. One of the less typical and highly popular versions of this traffic exchange for blogs is a site called 'mybloglog'.

Mybloglog as an internet marketing hotspot.

Mybloglog isn't JUST a traffic exchange – it provides 'a return on attention' – it is, in essence the bloggers blog tool. And for an internet marketer, its quite simply a community with leverage.

And as communities go, built around blogging, mybloglog is really quite cool. Owned by Yahoo, it does a great job of providing traffic, and growth to blogs.

And therein lies the rub.

You have to be very careful when using traffic exchanges to promote your blogs.

Most PPC based networks (unless you're lucky enough to run your own) frown on it – and some people have reported that they've been banned from ppc using it.

Even Yahoo's oddly.

Having said that, if your primary interest is traffic, you don't need to worry. mybloglog gives traffic until you're swamped. And its fairly targeted, as long as you categorise yourself properly.

Mybloglog's community is also a rather interesting place to hang out – you can pick up tips, tricks and find other blogs that are in your niche – again, you need to know where these people are, if only to know what your competitors and colleagues are doing.

Blogging is, when it comes down to it, a community 'thing' – you need a community around your blog for it to be a success, and on the whole, mybloglog provides the community aspect that most people need – at least to begin with.

OPB – other people's blogs

I've mentioned, while explaining a lot of this, that you should also know where your competitors are in relation to your blog.

Other people's blogs are also a great way to attract traffic – after all, they've already got people from your niche coming into their blog – the leg work is done – and the really big ones in your niche also have a nice secondary effect.

MOST blogs, when you comment on them, or comment about them and trackback (see the advanced strategies for more information on this!) will provide a link back to your blog, with your comment.

Sometimes its 'no follow' (a protocol introduced by Google et al. to combat spam) which means you don't get 'credit' in the search engines for your link back, but people can still click through to your blog. Its always of vital importance that if you're making a comment that you WANT associated with you that you include a link to your site. Each link has the potential for traffic, either coming to your blog to blast you for your view point (this is still good traffic, believe it or not – if the person cares enough to come over and challenge you, they may stay to read more) or to agree with you, which most times is where you'll pick up new readers from other people's blogs.

The people that agree with you, especially on controversial topics are automatically more likely to comment on your blog – and once someone opens a dialogue, they usually continue it.

That's not to say you should troll blogs to disagree with others. You shouldn't deliberately look for a reason to pick a fight on another blog – in fact, its usually good practice not to argue at all on blogs. If you truly believe the person blogging is presenting a 'fake' point of view, by all means call them on it. Lots of Big Dogs meet people doing that all the time, because its human nature to take a pop at something further up the food chain – but its important that you're doing it for all of the right reasons.

Though controversial conversations are the basis of strong blogging conversations, its also essential that you come away from them looking like a reasonable person, with understandable and approachable way. And as with everything else in blogging the keys to this are reasonable and approachable.

Passion is important, but tempered passion, and reasoned argument are usually the best way to attract people from controversial topics – after all, would YOU feel comfortable talking to someone that screams everyone else down?

Responding to Other Blogs

Controversy aside, there are some important etiquette points to pay attention to when responding to any blog post – or to comments on your own blog: Make sure you understand, fully, what the person is saying. You shouldn't respond to a comment in anger- it'll only lead to escalated tensions, and if something was said in a joking way, however unclear, you'll probably come off looking like the bad guy, even if that's not how YOU meant it. People perceive comments the way they expect the tone to be – so if its out of character for you, it will, generally look far worse.

Once you're ready to respond, you should stay on topic – or at least, start on topic, if you're responding on your blog.   If you're responding in the comments area, remember that its a small area and doesn't allow anywhere near as many words as you can fit in a blog post, so if its a LONG response, you should consider taking it, instead to your blog.   You should then always link back – blogger ad Wordpress both track these – bloggers calls them 'backlinks' and Wordpress calls them trackbacks (more about effective use of them in the 'advanced' section at the end of the book)

Ultimately, the person that owns the blog gets to decide whether to run your comment.   You can't force someone to post your comment and harassing them, again and again, will only lead to you being banned, and possibly named and shamed. Unless this blogger is an unreasonable person themselves, this will only lead to damage.

The bottom line to this is that the more readers you have, the more traffic you have – the more customers you should generate.

Step 6

The social networking and bookmarking debate.

So far, we've touched on the basics of commenting, blog marketing and mybloglog –
now we're going to go into slightly more advanced techniques for garnering readers.

Social networking and bookmarking has grown in popularity alongside blogging and
though not all of them are designed to be used with blogging, most of them are.

Example Site :

https://digg.com

Digg is, quite honestly, the mother ship when it comes to generating traffic from social
networking – you can be pretty much certain that if anyone makes it on Digg, they'll
soon be complaining.

NO server is designed to stream the loads that people see, after becoming a top Digg –
its quite likely that though most people hope and dream of seeing traffic like that,
you'll experience it once and think twice about ever attempting it again!
Digg is a great place to gain readers from certain niches – its a 'geeky' site, a lot like
Slashdot, and is designed to draw attention to the sites that are in those niches, with
worthwhile things to say. They do, however, have a business category, which means
Internet Marketers, with the right slant, can use Digg for bookmarking.

Digging someone is sort of like saying 'I recommend this' – its a global word of mouth script, and is very, very good. Every time someone 'recommends' or diggs you, you rise back up to the top of the front page, giving you a brief chance in the limelight. If you attract more attention there, you'll be dugg again, and again, and again, or you'll sink until someone else diggs you.

There is no time limit on Diggs – no statute of expiry. So its also a great way to get traffic to older posts – and probably most importantly, you can Digg yourself. You shouldn't use your Digg account only for that, but its perfectly acceptable to submit your own site to Digg, occasionally.

The community can't – really – be gamed all that well, because its so vast, but there are ways to cheat at every social bookmarking site – Digg is SO huge though that many people find they just get...buried.

Like every community, it is, in part about friendships – the gaming effect would be really easy if everyone voted for everyone else, but, to be quite honest, most people vote for the stuff that really interests them. So once you hook them as a reader they WILL vote.

There's also no harm (whatsoever) in encouraging your readership, as it grows, to digg you, to bookmark you on delicious, or to add you to other sites – there are plugins and widgets designed specifically for that purpose – just make sure your traffic is voting for the best of your material, and you'll garner even more readers.

The main thing about Digg is its like a snowball. Gain enough momentum and people will continue to vote for you and you'll keep popping right back up to the top.

Step 7

Tying it all up

The seventh day to blogging is a relatively short one – is everything you're doing, working so far?

You won't be able to evaluate traffic, but you should have a comfortable grasp of what you're going to be doing with your blog, and possibly a few fledgling commenters'.

From here on in you should be scheduling regular posting, and regular interaction on other blogs, in communities and forums, and of course, most of all, planning a strategy for continuing the building blocks you've started.

You won't know – yet – where the best bookmarking sites for you are – nor will you be able to decide whether your keywords are appropriate as yet. You WILL, however, know how easily you've found your first week, and you will be able to adapt your project overview accordingly.

You should also decide at this point, where you want to focus properly. Do you want to post daily – and can you commit to that? DO you feel posting less often will allow you to build a stronger, fluff free blog, without over committing? OR would once a week be enough?

Whatever you decide, after the first week or two, you NEED to be consistent. You should find a routine to settle into and then work towards continuing that schedule for as long as possible.

It IS possible to make money from a blog, but those blogs are at the top of their field, and this is simply because they are the best in their niche, blogs wise. As long as you aim for the best quality you can possibly produce, comfortably, you can't go wrong. It may take you a while to attract traffic, but if, in a month, you're still struggling to bring people in, you should review that side of your blogging.

While great content is the cornerstone of the best blogs – they also have a certain amount of focus on traffic driving. At critical mass (when that traffic brings in its OWN traffic) you can relax a bit on that side, but it takes a while to get there.

You should always keep an eye on what works, and what doesn't though, because eliminating that will leave you with a leaner, stronger blog than people that don't pay attention to these things, giving you a definitive edge over your competition.

And beyond?

One month on.

Is your blog outperforming your expectations?

Every marketing strategy needs reviewed every once in a while. You'll need to tweak, to adjust, and most of all, lose the bits that you're getting nothing from.

Step One: Keep Track of Your Blog Results

Tracking your blogs stats is as simple as ABC.

First though, you've got to work out what you want to track. Do you want to track your traffic? Do you care more about comments? How about what you're earning...

Primary goal – traffic

Keeping track of your traffic is as easy as finding a stats program you like and using it. There's a great one built into Cpanel called Awstats, or you could use

https://analytics.google.com

Either way, you have to understand how to read the statistics.

Awstats is reasonably easy to understand – the most important two numbers in it are the unique visitors and your page views. You might also want to see who is bookmarking you – in the sense of coming back to visit you using a simple 'bookmark me' function in their browser.

Bookmarking beyond the simple 'favourite' concept.

Favouriting a site, or bookmarking it, is the act of saving the URL in a list that you can then access from a menu in your browser. But in recent years there's also been another way to bookmark a site – and that way is interestingly, to drive boatloads of traffic to your site, if used correctly.

Its most important to remember that this form of 'bookmarking' was initially based on the browser based lists we keep on our own pc's – designed around allowing you to 'share' your favourites with others.

And then sites like Digg, Technorati and Delicious sprung up, giving people a broad range of ways to mark out the best items in another blog – sharing it, with everyone that's interested in the niche of the bookmarked blogs. If you're using social bookmarking, you should also try to keep track of roughly how well it's working out for you – how many 'diggs' you're receiving, how much traffic its referring in. You should be able to see that in your stats too, by looking for URL's that refer from the sites that you're bookmarked on. If your website stats are doing their job, they WILL track this.

Once you know how well your traffic is performing, you can decide which content is driving the BEST traffic. If you've got a goal for your blog, be it making money, referrals, or simply driving traffic to your other site, you can use your traffic (and affiliate stats/earnings) to find out which posts are drawing the most traffic and work on extending on those results.

One month in you should have several 'cornerstone' posts that define the whole concept of your blog – giving your readers several strong posts that give both the tone and nature of your blog. These cornerstone posts should be among your strongest performing posts, or you should work on making a couple of stronger ones. These cornerstone posts can also be used, one month in (to give them plenty of time to index in search engines), as articles in sites like **https://ezinearticles.com** – giving you even MORE traffic coming in from relevant sites.

Advanced techniques

Feed Burner

Feed Burner is a great way to add additional options to your site, not limited to subscription boxes, portable feed results, reposting of your information (for example, syndicating your articles is possible just by giving people your Feed Burner code. Their site updates automatically, and you control where they are clicking through to if they are interested in what you are saying in your articles. Its win – win).

Feed Burner was recently bought out by Google, giving you several amazing new options – including opening up their Pro services.
Most people use a lot of the Feed Burner functions, so its highly recommended that you grab your own account and explore.

Advanced techniques with Feed Burner also include the ability to 'fix' feeds so that they are readable, and track your feed stats.

Once you've set up your feed in Feed Burner keep the URL handy.

AWeber

If you've fed your Blogger atom feed through Feed Burner this will also work, but Wordpress has feeds that work well with one of the most amazing things that AWeber offers for bloggers, and one of the main reasons I use AWeber.

AWeber has a facility that allows you to attach your blog feed to your email list, giving you the opportunity to email your list the instant you update your blog. This is a great way to automate some of your posting process. And all it takes is filling in a form in AWeber, and putting a subscription form on your site. Not so advanced really.

You'll also be able to set up a template for your posts at the same time – you can choose one of dozens of templates that can compliment your site.

There is in fact, only one caveat to all of this.

If you post multiple times a day, you run the risk of annoying people – and if you don't post enough, your 'newsletters' may not be issued often enough. So you've got to set it up to post at regular intervals, which is where this gets slightly complicated.

Optimal posting is once a week – BUT...if you've got time critical information, this might not work out well for you.

So, you need to work out how to get AWeber to send out an email once a week – if your average posting schedule is three posts a week, set it up to post your information every four posts – add one to your week's post UNLESS you only post once a week – in which case, set it to send once per week.

You'll also still be able to send 'broadcasts' announcing any time critical information – and you'll STILL be able to set up your auto responses to your list – effectively offering you 'triple duty' on your autoresponders.

Other autoresponders may not offer this service so you'll need to check with them.

If your business is more list driven than blog driven, you can also take your list and post it to your blog. You'll need to find a plugin that works with your program – and this does not (as far as I'm aware) work with Blogger.

Trackbacks

There are more ways than one to pay regard to a good blogger – if you're linking to – or someone is linking to you, MOST blogs will track this.

Its called 'tracking back' – or backlinking in blogger – or, sometimes even pinging.

It is the art of linking back to a blog that you've read, and referenced – but more than that, its a way to get an effortless link BACK from a blog that YOU read, as long as they accept trackbacks.

Its an advanced technique, because you can't just 'trackback' to from any post – its important to choose only one, two or at a maximum, three blog posts to link back to.

When linking back, you have to use a special link, in the case of WordPress, its simply got 'trackback' on the end.

You use the 'regular' link in the post – this 'regular' link would be exactly the same one as you use to access the single post – you then put /trackback/ on the end of this, and place it in the box designated trackbacks.

As far as I'm aware, Blogger has no option to do this, but might automatically post them.

No matter what you do with your blog, you'll always find that you can get more traffic, more interest, and more eyeballs to your site with a blog.

And no matter how you work on your blog, if you follow our pattern, you'll find that in a month you can make a huge impact on your website.

"To Your Greater Success" !

Email List Building

(For Your Blog)

How To Generate Leads. Many Strategies To Grow Your Email List Quickly. A Step by Step Guide For Beginners To Launching a Successful Small Business.

(BONUS 4) – FREE BOOK - By : "Santiago Johnson Smith"

TABLE OF CONTENTS [BONUS 4 – EMAIL LIST BUILDING] :

Description

Chapter 1: Search Engine Optimization

Chapter 2: Using Article Marketing

Chapter 3: Paid E-zine Advertising

Chapter 4: Pay-Per-Click Programs

Chapter 5: The Value Of A Press Release

Chapter 6: Using Special Reports To Kick Start

Chapter 7: Compound List Building with Resell Rights

Chapter 8: Using The Ad Swap

Chapter 9: The Magic of Give-Away Events

Chapter 10: Investing in Co-Registration Leads

Chapter 11: Recruiting an Army of Affiliates

Chapter 12: Leveraging on Joint Ventures

Chapter 13: Executing Product Launches

Description

Tired Of Looking For New Customers & Yearning For Residual Income Streams?

Discover How YOU - Or Anyone - Can Quickly & Easily Create Your Very Own Recurring Income Generating Asset Online...

Allowing YOU To Increase Profits From Your Repeat Customers While Building Your Own Expert Status & Credibility In The Process!"

Dear Internet Entrepreneur,

Perhaps you're here because you are still seeking the *right answers* for your Internet business and you need them fast... or perhaps because your business is still really struggling for success.

Let's work together on changing all of that today!

You probably already know the secret to creating recurring riches online... You know, the one that allows you to make money at will and pull in sale after sale, just like clockwork?

Yep, you have probably guessed it: it's having a responsive mailing list.

You can build your own database of prospects... and then build a relationship with them so that they *want* to say subscribed to your list.

You can remind them about your main product that you are selling on your web site... and invite them to return for another look. You can make important announcements so these prospects can visit your site **and then, sell them even more of your products!**

These are just some of the ideas, but you get what I mean, right?

"But It's Often Easier Said Than Done, Isn't It?"

Well, that's list building for you. It's only easy to do if you know the techniques that really work.

Quickly And Easily Build & Grow Your Online Mailing List For Maximum Profits!" And I leave NO stone unturned in this section... because I want you to be able to absorb and USE these valuable tactics right away!

Discover 6 totally different and unique strategies that you can easily execute right now and build your mailing list from scratch! It doesn't matter if you have only a few hundred subscribers or even 0 - these methods can be carried out right away!

What you get:

* A killer technique that can enable you to double or even triple your list building results using any of these tenderfoot techniques alone!

* How to get TARGETED traffic funnelled in from major Search Engines online FREE!

* How to use articles to build your mailing list and establish yourself as an authority figure in any niche of your choosing!

* How to earn decent returns from paid advertising online - I show you how NOT to waste money in lousy advertising PLUS show you how to identify paid advertising revenue that really works!

* What it takes to achieve MAXIMUM opt-in rates from your list building campaigns!

* How to drive in laser-focused traffic from popular Search Engines with little investment, MAJOR returns!

* How to use online/offline media to build your database of responsive prospects without having to risk being too "sales pitchy" and resorting to hype in the process!

* Create your vital credibility and then your mailing list through this popular vehicle as used by TOP marketing gurus from around the planet!

* And much more!

Chapter 1: Search Engine Optimization

A Short Introduction...

Thank you for investing your time in this special course, which is likened to the key to your list building success! List building is very, very critical to the success of any business online or offline. And it applies to your success whether you own a small, medium or big-sized business.

Brick-n-mortar companies invest a great effort in collecting prospective leads.

Network Marketers often begin with writing a list of 100 names of people they know. And as an Online Business owner, you should focus on building your Online Mailing List.

Now list building isn't exactly a riddle... as long as you know what to do, and how to do it. Incidentally, that is the aim of this book - to show you how to get started on building your mailing list using multiple, unique and different techniques that add TARGETED leads to your database at as low cost as possible. Yet you can profit wildly in the process.

As more than one technique is discussed in this book, you have my word that at least one or more techniques would suit you - or anyone. Of course, it would be wiser to practice more than one list building technique simultaneously to observe greater results.

Without further ado, let's move on with the first tenderfoot list building technique... Without a doubt, one of the most effective ways in which you, as a website owner, can set up a potential list of clients is to build an email list of those who visit.

SEO (Search Engine Optimization) Introduced By being able to better interact on a more "one on one" platform, you can quickly convert those who would otherwise simply browse around on your website and then leave, into potential sales and money in your pocket.

The profit potential does not stop there though, as with a well-constructed email list filled with people from all walks of life, you can even entice your subscribers to visiting your website more often than they normally would - setting you up to enhance your site's moneymaking ability even more through various advertisements.

So as you can see, the email list is one of the most important tools in any webmaster's repertoire and if you want your online business, no matter what it is, to be as successful as possible then you will need to spend a lot of time perfecting that email list.

Now, you are probably thinking that sure, an email list is great, but let's not get ahead of ourselves - there are many more steps to be done before we can actually start directly marketing to people on an email list.

SEO - Step-by-Step :

First, we actually have to get the visitors to our website before we can even dream of adding them to our mailing lists.

A few years back with the rise of popular search engines like Yahoo and Google, a group of cunning marketers, probably not unlike yourself, decided that the best way to get random people and potential customers to visit their websites was to take advantage of search engine technology.

They figured that if you could code a website and write content for it that designed with the sole purpose of moving that page's status in any given search engine to the top, then they would be able to receive far more visitors than anyone ever thought possible.

In today's web design world, the theory of search engine optimization, or SEO as it is often referred to, is an extremely popular topic among web designers and online business owners from all walks of life - no matter what they are selling or if they are even selling anything at all.

With so many competing websites in your chosen field or niche the only hope that you may have to rise above the seventeenth page of Google is to make sure that your website is as optimized for search engines as it can possibly be.

Because SEO is so popular these days there are hundreds of different websites out there that claim they have the answers to make sure that your page is among the top ten on all of the big three search engines: Yahoo, MSN and Google. However, if you take these tips and tricks on their own, you will quickly discover that there are far too many for you to take in. Perhaps the case is that everyone thinks they have the solution to the SEO problem - but nobody really does, so they just make things up hoping they will attract more visitors to their own websites. Therefore, when scouring the World Wide Web for all sorts of information on how to make sure that your website is optimized for search engines, it is a great idea to compare and contrast the information you find at one website with the information you find at others.

Comparing and contrasting is tedious though, so to get you started, we have already done a bit of the tough legwork for you so you can jump right onto the SEO bandwagon and get your email lists up and running in no time.

Search Engine Optimization Tips :

The first of our comprehensive SEO tips for those looking to establish their own mailing lists is to make sure that your website is as straightforward as it possibly can be.

Anything that deviates from the ordinary, whether it be Adobe Flash integration, crazy layout schemes or the use of dynamic URLs for certain pages under your domain can be disastrous to the budding web designer who is trying to take advantage of SEO for the first time.

Secondly, be specific with the keywords that you select for your website. Far too often, a person who is looking to get into optimization will select a perfectly good keyword but it will be far too general.

What you are looking for are specific keywords, keywords that are searched relatively often but lack the heavy competition of more generic keywords. After all, suppose you put "book" in as your keyword.

That's all well and good, but to be perfectly honest, your website will probably never compete with the likes of Amazon or Barnes and Noble, so be more specific. Consider something more along the lines of "antique book," "first run book" or something like that instead. Finally, be sure to direct your entire website to the optimization cause.

If you want to bring in the traffic (and keep potential customers around for a while) you will have to have great content. That is a no-brainer. But did you know that you can make other parts of your website work for you too? Yes, take advantage of adding your chosen keywords to the header portion of your HTML document, make the titles of your website contain the keyword too, and do not forget to use the "alt" image tags to proudly display your chosen keywords as well. After you think you have a fully mature search engine optimized website up and running, your next step should be to focus on your mailing list. Tweak and tune your content to make sure that it is good enough to make people stick around on your website and offer visitors something that will make them want to join your mailing list.

Promise to give people on your mailing lists essential updates, one time only offers, or whatever else you think is good enough to make them sign up to your email list. Often, the most creative ideas are the most successful, so go wild with your ideas and you will have a successful email list in no time.

Chapter 2: Using Article Marketing

How many different email marketing lists do you belong to? If your mailbox is anything like mine, then you probably have subscribed yourself to quite a few during your browsing sessions online.

Whether the emails that you get are from other businesses that may be able to provide you with goods or services that you simply cannot get anywhere else for the price, for musicians who you like to keep an eye on in hopes that they will visit your city sometime soon or from bloggers who have great articles in your eyes - your email box is probably filled to the brim with notifications that you subscribed to at some point or another.

Now that you are considering moving into the realm of the online business, it is high time that you learn to take advantage of the power of an email list and notification program.

Potential clients and random visitors alike love notification lists, as it keeps them up to date on what you've got going on without them having to visit your website every moment of every day.

People like things to be easy - and that is exactly what an email list is giving them - easy access to information on your website when they want it.

At this point in your career as a blossoming webmaster, you probably do not know too much about the whole web design thing. However, even with your potential lack of experience, you have probably realized that it takes a well-designed website with some killer content to draw people in and make them stick around.

While terms like article marketing and SEO may elude you, it does not take a rocket scientist to realize that you have got to have good, enjoyable, enlightening information on your website to make your guests want to stick around - and one of the best ways to do so is to be involved in an article marketing program.

So What Exactly Is Article Marketing?

Quite simply it is just as it sounds - marketing your articles and taking advantage of articles written by other people to bring traffic to your own website. Because of the definition, there are two very different ways in which you can become a part of the article marketing phenomenon.

Submitting or using:

Whichever method of article marketing your prefer is entirely up to you, although the former is much better way to attract traffic to your website and the latter should only be used in extreme situations.

Thanks to the wondrous power of the article marketing websites, there has never been a better time for you than now to become a better writer. Writing Articles For Business Marketing - You see, in order to be able to take advantage of the amazing marketing potential of submitting to an article marketing website, you first have to be able to write your own articles.

For some people who truly enjoy writing content all day long, this will not be a problem as they will be able to crank out great content in no time and flood the article marketing websites with lots of cool articles that everyone will want to have on their websites - easily getting their names out there so that they can start to establish a comprehensive email list of potential clients.

However, there is that problem that many people face who simply cannot draft an enjoyable document if their life depends on it. If you are one of those types of people, the road to establishing an email list through article marketing will be long and arduous.

Eventually, you will be able to write an article that you deem worthy of submitting to an article marketing website. After some time you may even get a few hits on it and a few unique visitors to your website because of it.

But how much time are you willing to spend on something that may only net you a couple of people on your email list? Instead, why not try hiring a freelance writer.

There are droves of them out there in cyberspace who will work for relatively cheap rates and provide you with decent content (and if you don't like what they have provided you with, you can always edit it).

Although many article marketing websites require that you write the articles yourself, if you have a ghost-writer do the dirty work for you, you can claim the article as your own and nobody will be the wiser.

Submitting To Article Directories :

Once your article writing is finished, it is time to submit your work to an article marketing website. After it has been up there for a while you will start to see people view it and you may even get a few downloads here or there.

It is the downloads that you are really looking for, as it shows that someone found it interesting enough to put it on their website using your name, link, and email address so that people will know who actually wrote the article in the first place bringing your website traffic. Below, you will find a comprehensive list of some of the better article sites on the Internet. There are literally hundreds of sites, but these are the ones you could start with.

List Of Article Directories :

Article City
https://www.articlecity.com

Article Finders
https://scholar.google.com

Articles Factory

http://articlesfactory.com

Articles Network

http://articlesnetwork.com

Constant Content

https://www.constant-content.com

Go Articles

https://ezinearticles.com

How To Advice

http://howtoadvice.com

Idea Marketers

https://www.ideamarketers.com

Morgan Article Archive

http://morganarticlearchive.com

The Ezine Dot Net

https://www.theezine.net

Certificate.net

https://certificate.net

Now, you can also use other peoples' articles on your own website if you must, but remember that you have to provide plenty of links to the original author's website - a risk that can possibly drive people away from your own website before they are able to enrol in your email list.

Getting people onto your email list through an article marketing plan can be tricky and arduous, but for the most part it is one of the more successful methods for establishing a good client base.

A lot of work must be done before you even think about posting that first article on an article marketing site, but once you are through with that all you have to do is sit back and watch as it brings in more and more potential customers to your website.

With each unique visit, there is another chance that person could sign up for your email list. And we all know that the more people on your email list at the end of the day, the more people you can sell to in order to maximize your profits.

Chapter 3: Paid E-zine Advertising

Building a comprehensive email list is one of the most beneficial techniques afforded to webmasters and online business owners these days.

There is perhaps no better way to establish a massive database of potential clients than through an email list that contains the names and email addresses of many who have passed through your site.

However, the problem remains that people must first visit your website before they are able to sign up to your email list, and even the most novice of us know that driving an abundant amount of unique traffic to our website can be a daunting task.

Luckily enough, there are many ways of getting the traffic that we all desire. Some of these ways are free but may take a bit longer to amass hordes of people while other methods require you to pay a fee up front but seem to work a bit faster.

Whichever you decide is totally up to how much you feel you can make in your online business and how much you are willing to spend in an attempt to gain as much traffic - and as long of a mailing list, as you possibly can.

Paid Advertising Explained:

Of the paid for methods of building your own email list and bringing gobs of traffic to your website, possibly the most successful is through paid e-zine advertising techniques.

The e-zine is a relatively obscure topic for most people, and chances are that unless you are really into marketing and advertising you have never heard the name "e-zine" mentioned before now.

Essentially an e-zine is basically an electronic magazine that is published by a particular website.

Different than a mailing list, an e-zine is usually tightly linked to a particular topic or subject, so that everyone who has access to a particular ezine is interested in that one topic.

There are unique e-zines for just about anything out there from how to build a successful website to how to find the best shoes to where are some of the best destinations for people who like to travel by boat.

The possibilities for different types of e-zines are endless, so the first step in any paid e-zine advertising plan should be to find and research the different types of e-zines that will fit into your site's niche.

Sourcing Out For The Best Paid E-zine Advertising:

Once you find a particular e-zine that you feel is the right media for your advertisements, you should contact the owner of the e-zine and see if he is open to the idea of you sticking your advertisements in the e-zine itself.

If the e-zine owner is open to the idea of paid advertising, then you are good to go and you should start creating some advertisements immediately.

On the other hand, if for some reason the owner of the e-zine is not interested in sticking your advertisements in (for any price) then you should simply move on to another e-zine that is also well suited to your business.

Creating Your Own Advertisements:

Now comes the tricky part for any potential paid e-zine advertiser looking to enhance the membership of their budding email list - creating the advertisements themselves.

The ads you make will have to be more than simple content if you want to unleash the full power of a paid e-zine advertisement.

Remember that hundreds, thousands or sometimes millions of people will be viewing the e-zine with your advertisement in it, and if you want a decent majority of those people to actually click your link, visit your website and subsequently sign up for your email list, then you will have to be especially clever with your advertisements.

Even more so if you find that there are multiple advertisers competing with you in the same e-zine issue.

Many people at this point will probably think that their best shot for successful paid e-zine advertisements will be to advertise exactly what their website does, and why someone should pay any attention to it.

Unfortunately, while this may be decent for some people, it is a practice that has proven to be unsuccessful for those looking to build an email list. After all, if a person knows exactly what they are getting from your web service, then why would they want to visit your advertisement if they weren't interested in your services?

That is all well and good if you are selling only one particular product, but you want to craft an email list.

So instead you need an ad that will piqué their interest in what you offer something that will make them want to visit your website, sign up for your email list and come back for more again and again. This is the only way that you will find yourself able to maximize the payout from a paid e-zine advertisement if you are trying to create your own email list.

The Maximum Opt-In Conversion Rate Solution The solution to maximizing email list subscriptions through the use of a paid ezine advertisement is to give the people what they want - something for free or your services in a risk-free offer.

Whatever it is that you offer them for free is totally up to you, and in all honesty it does not really matter so long as you give only a rough idea of what your potential customers are getting for free in the advertisement.

You can give away anything from a free article to free research to a free one week subscription to whatever services you are trying to peddle. Just make sure that you let everyone reading the advertisement that if they visit your website they will be entitled to something cool totally free of charge. Now, just make sure that the e-zine advertisement you have created points directly to your email list sign-up page, tell your visitors that they have to enrol in your email list to receive the free gift and you are all set.

Oh, and be sure that at some point you do actually follow through with giving the people who sign up for your mailing list or you may have a few angry people in the following days. And there you have it, the start of your brand new email list as only paid e-zine advertising can provide!

Chapter 4: Pay-Per-Click Programs

If you want your website, online business or blog to be as successful as it possibly can be, and to be honest - who doesn't? Then what you need is a comprehensive mailing list with names and email addresses of all sorts of people to market your products or services to.

Since most visitors to any given website do not make a purchase on their first browse, it is of the utmost importance that you keep track of as many visitors as you can with an email list. That way, you can more directly market to them later on and convert that marketing energy into sales to generate you profit.

Making the hard sale the first time out is extremely difficult, so use an email list to let the buyers come to you - and then grab them when they are ready to purchase something from you.

The email list marketing tactic works for just about any kind of online (or brick and mortar) business, whether you are selling products, doing custom research for people or writing articles that they can use on their own websites. In order to build an email list that you can later use to solicit your products, you first have to drum up some visitors to your website. This is actually the most difficult part of the task because there is so much competition out there for just about any website.

Even if you think your website is so unique and different from anything else out there, I can almost guarantee you that you will have at least ten other sources of direct competition for your same market - making it harder for people to pick out your website when there are others that may be just as good (in their eyes) as yours. Although search engine optimization and article marketing are viable methods of generating traffic for your website, if you really want to rake in the traffic to build a huge email list, you will have to consider using a pay-for method like pay per click advertising or paid e-zine advertisements.

Sure, neither of these marketing techniques come cheap - but if you can add even a handful of the visitors you get from these campaigns to your email list, then a pay for advertising method will be totally worth it.

Pay-Per-Click Exposed!

Thanks to the success of the search engine business in the past few years, the pay per click advertising method seems to be the best payoff for someone looking to generate traffic and build their own email list. Because so many people frequent search engines like Google and Yahoo each and every day, pay per click advertising is the perfect way for you to get unique visitors to stop by your website - even if search engine optimization techniques have not been able to bump your website up to the first page yet. So, if you are interested in gaining the best benefit for your buck in terms of visitors to your website, then paying Google or Yahoo each time someone clicks on your ad is well worth it.

How It Works:

Each and every time someone clicks on your ad, you will have to pay a small amount of money to the company you purchased the ad space with, but if you are turning most of those visits into sales or valuable additions to your email list, then the fee will be well worth it.

Google is one of the biggest names in the search engine business and their ability to bring in visitors to all sorts of different websites should not be taken lightly.

With well-placed Google pay per click advertisements, just about any web business owner can turn his downtrodden website into a moneymaking bonanza in a matter of weeks.

Thanks to their ingenious AdWords program, Google will be happy to give you a plethora of pay per click advertising space on the results page of peoples' searches to advertising sections on other peoples' websites.

Yes, with a contract with AdWords you can be well on your way to getting visitors left and right. However, as with all things that seem so great, there is a catch with Google AdWords - you have to work long and hard on choosing the right keywords for your website.

The special algorithm used by AdWords only shows a few relevant ads based on keywords, so if you are unsuccessful in choosing the right keywords for the most effectively targeted ads, then you will be left with far fewer visitors to your domain than you though.

The other promising choice for those looking to get into pay per click advertisement as a way to get visitors to their website for email list purposes is to use Yahoo's Search Marketing (formerly known as Overture) service.

Since this service has been around much longer than Google's AdWords, it is much more robust in terms of what you can do with it.

While AdWords is much more focused on targeted advertisements, with Yahoo Search Marketing you can actually target your ads by different criteria - not just by the keywords you have chosen to use. This gives you as an online business owner much more flexibility over who gets to view your ads and when they get to view them.

Now that you have been acquainted with the top two names in the pay per click advertising marketplace, you should be better prepared to make a decision about how you want to go about attracting visitors to your website.

With pay per click advertisements, you do not have to worry about spending money frivolously on ads because you never have to pay anyone until somebody clicks on the ad for your website. Furthermore, with both Google and Yahoo, you actually get to name your own price for how much you pay per click - making pay per click advertising a feasible method of generating website traffic even for those webmasters on a tight budget.

As one final tip for anyone looking to get into pay per click advertising as a way of building an email list, make sure that your advertisement is linked directly to your email list signup page, as you cannot expect people who have visited your website via an ad click to browse around for long.

Chapter 5: The Value Of A Press Release

Building a successful website can be tricky business - especially if you have plans to make that website the crux of your income statements each year.

After all, with so many other websites out there that are probably selling the same or similar goods and services as you, what is there to set your business apart from the pack?

One simple answer should be the contents of your website. People like a nice, clean design for the sites that they frequent and they like to have plenty of enjoyable articles or copy to read that is genuinely interesting to them.

If you are able to supply those two fundamental features you will be well on your way to making your online business thrive. But what if you want to take that extra step to make your website into a moneymaking machination?

There is one simple tool that you can employ if you want to ensure that you will get more people to purchase from you - create an email list that potential customers and current customers can sign up for.

The mailing list allows you to do something that most stores wish they could do: attract visitors and then market products to them on their schedules so the hard sale does not seem so hard to swallow in their eyes.

Even with a small email list you will have a much higher rate of sales than if you were to forgo the email list all together, so what do you say - perhaps it is high time that you create one for your website. Unfortunately we cannot go around and simply collect random names and email addresses to add to our email lists, so it is up to us to first generate enough traffic for our website and then convert those visitors into email list subscribers.

There are tons of different ways in which you can get traffic to come – some ways, like pay per click advertising cost you some money while other like search engine optimization are totally free so long as you know what you are doing.

However, both of these techniques are totally passive. Try as you might, it may take you weeks or months before you actually see any of these techniques come to fruition as actual inquiries on your email list.

Instead, if you want to grab the proverbial bull by the horns and rake in people by the droves right away then you will have to do something a bit more drastic.

Bring In Press Releases!

That something is a tried and true technique that has been employed by businesses of all types for centuries. Known as the press release, you can use this method to drive people to your website almost instantaneously the moment someone picks up and publishes the release.

At this point you are probably thinking that such a technique is too good to be true and would be impossible for a lowly online business owner like yourself – but the good news is that anyone can draft a press release and submit it to many of the major daily publications, both online and print based. All it takes is a little bit of time and some know-how of what you need to include in your particular press release.

Drafting Out Your Press Release:

The first aspect of a press release that you need to concentrate on is the actual content of that release itself. Nobody wants to read some drab, boring press release - and certainly nobody will want to publish it in their periodical, so consider jazzing it up to include a lot of content that people who would be interested in your website would want to hear. Include facts, figures, statistics and even plans of action for what you and your business plan to do in the future in an attempt to get people to check out your website.

Remember: no sales pitch, too! People expect something newsworthy from you. While you should make the content as interesting to your potential customers as possible, it is important not to lie, since chances are that your potential clients will check up on you over time to make sure that you are wholly backing up what you say in press releases with what you actually do. Also, when writing the content, be sure to address your possible clients personally instead of addressing them as some vague demographic as far too many press releases tend to do. This will make the reader feel more at home and will likely make him or her more inclined to visit your website.

Secondly, if you plan on submitting your press release to mostly websites who will publish it, then you should try to optimize it for search engines as much as possible.

Remember that the more aligned your press release is with certain keywords the more it will be read by people who could be your potential customers and subscribers to your new email list, and the better it will be for your business in the long term.

Please though, do not overuse the keywords you have decided to focus on, as it will make for a very dry, boring and uninteresting press release that certainly will not allow you to get the maximum number of visitors.

Finally, once your press release has been written and edited, you will want to find some spots to post it. I recommend these (but there are many more if you 'google' the term):

https://www.prweb.com
https://www.newswire.com
https://www.imnewswatch.com
https://www.pr.com/press-releases

Be sure to get into contact with places that you know will be able to distribute your press release to the masses, but also try and find some avenues of distribution that take advantage of RSS or Atom feeds. Using RSS or Atom will allow your press release to be sent directly to the masses like the top headlines for the New York Times or Google News and is a great way for your business to take advantage of technology in the pursuit for a massive email list.

So there you have it, the basics for using a press release to gain as many visitors to your website as possible. Since you are looking to establish an email list from many of those visitors, be sure to have the link from your press release pointing to your subscription list page, as you do not want people to dawdle around on your website and lose interest before they sign up for your email list. Do this, and you will quickly find that your website will be successful in much less time than you ever thought possible!

Chapter 6: Using Special Reports To Kick Start

Your Campaign Marketing is about contacts, and in today's business world, emails are as valuable as just about any contact you can have. The key, though, is not just to have a list of emails; it is to have a list of qualified emails that you can turn into clients and profits.

Certainly getting a list of qualified email contacts sounds great, but how do you do it? There are a number of ways to get qualified emails, but one of the most effective ways is through the special report.

When used properly, the special report can give you and your business credibility while helping you to build an email list of qualified potential clients.

Take a look at the information below and you will quickly be on your way to building your business through an email list created from a special report.

Creating a Report About Your Subject:

Perhaps the best way to encourage perspective clients and customers subscribe to your e-zine or email list is to provide them with relevant and useful information. Your special report allows you to provide something of value (information) to your prospects without discounting your product or giving anything away.

Before you can start to use your special report, you obviously will need to create one. This is the most important part of the process, because if the report is not put together correctly, its effectiveness will be compromised even if you do everything else exactly right.

Start by considering niche topics that will benefit your prospective clients. If you offer real and useful information, those who read the report will be more likely to opt into your email list in hopes of gaining access to more useful information from you down the road.

If your report is not useful, prospects will be less likely to read the report and even if they do it may not result in the email opt-in even 'sticking with you' and with whom you are hoping to build your email list.

Secondly, research your special report heavily and make sure that your information is rich. Good content will bring opt-ins while bad content will just disgruntle prospects and leave you with a bad report and no emails.

Finally, proofread and edit heavily. Your content should be smooth, well written, and easy to understand. Good information that is easy to understand makes you look good.

On the other hand, good information with lots of errors and that is difficult to understand will may make you look inept. Have several sets of eyes look over your special report before you move on.

Turning Your Report Into A PDF Document:

The next step, once you have written your special report, is to have it converted into a PDF document. PDF files have a more professional look and can make you look technologically savvy to your customers.

What's more, they will look exactly the way you designed them no matter what the hardware or software is that the recipient uses. Converting your special report into a PDF document is simple, so the amount of work you put in versus the payoff is profound.

There are a few ways to convert your file into PDF format, and one way is to find a reliable and free online converter (Adobe.com has one) or you can download a software product to use on your own computer. Using your favorite search engine, you can find numerous free software applications that will convert any printable file into a PDF file. If you are only doing a few special reports, this is the fastest way.

I recommend:

https://www.primopdf.com or https://openoffice.org for the job, but there are several others, as well. There are many options out there, so do your homework and find the one that works best for your business.

The important thing here is to make sure you get a clean conversion and that your special report looks professional and just the way you designed it.

Circulating Your Report:

You have created a special report on a topic that you know about and that pertains to your target clientele. That is great, but now you have to make sure that they are actually looking at the report.

If nobody reads your report, it obviously won't do you any good. So then how do you get your special report circulating and working for you?

First and foremost, make sure it is well known within your company. It should appear on your website as a download and your employees should have links to the download location on their email signatures.

This will give your existing clientele access to the special report and anyone with which your employees have contact: a nice start.

The second way to circulate your special report is to write shorter content that will appear online where your prospects are looking.

Write a small article that leads to the information in your report, add a link to the report at the end, and post the articles on content websites and even message boards. Spread the word through the industry that you have something of value for free.

Finally, create a flier or other print advertising for your special report. Include the location (a link) for the special report and make your flier available at conferences, conventions, and any other event where you may encounter potential clients. Getting the word out every way possible will assure that plenty of eyeballs are finding your report.

Building an Email List from Your Report:

Once you have a useful report with good content, and once you have properly marketed that report so that it is in front of potential clients, you need to get emails from them.

The email list you are about to build is the main reason you created your special report in the first place. So how do you build an email list from your report? If you have put together an effective and valuable special report, then your clients will want to give you their email. Your job is to make sure there is a way for them to do that.

Within your special report, offer opportunities to get more information from you by opting into your email list. Offer an e-zine or other information to potential clients who do so.

Provide links to your company website on most if not all pages of your special report. At your site, make sure opting into the email list is easy to do, convenient, and quick.

If your target sees something he or she likes, it should be convenient to get to your site and to sign up for your email list. Remember that the report needs to stand alone as both an informative special report and as a marketing tool to help you collect qualified email leads.

This is important as you allow the report to be resold and passed along by others in the industry.

A Valuable Tool:

As you can see, using a special report can be a great way to build your email list. What's more, you will find that there are many things you can do to make your special report an ongoing aid in the maintenance and continual building of your list.

Just remember to make the content good, the report valuable, and the opt-in process convenient and you will have a qualified and reliable list in no time!

This Ends Part One...

This pretty much sums up the basic techniques of list building. While there are obviously more advanced list building techniques that you can practice and use for your own, I thought you should know that many a top marketer are making it big online today using even some of these "basic" methods to build their list... to a great extent!

You now know what it takes to build your mailing list from scratch, and I would advice you to test every one of them to see what works best for you. This is because every individual is different.

Therefore there are some methods that would work especially better than the other for you. Are you ready for the 'intermediate list-building' training section now?

Chapter 7: Compound List Building with Resell Rights

As you may well know by now from the last chapter in Ultimate List Builder's Course, creating special reports is a great way to market your business.

You can use those reports to build your credibility, raise the awareness of your company, and acquire qualified lists of emails for potential clients.

In order to truly spread your special report around, which is how you get the most benefit from it, you should look into granting resale permission for the report.

Once you have written your special report, you have to find a way to make sure that people are actually reading it.
After all, getting people to read your special report is the only way to reap the other benefits of writing one.

As you will see, there is a lot to be gained from resale permissions.

In addition to that, it is easy to get started once you have written your special report. Finally, you will see that your email list may just be the biggest winner in the resale permission game.

What is Resale Permission?

You may have heard the phrase "resale permission" before, but it is possible that you didn't know what it meant.

Basically, if you grant resale permission on a special report you wrote, you are giving another person or company permission to sell or distribute your report and collect any profits for themselves entirely.

While that sounds like a great deal for the person to whom you grant permission, it is also a pretty good deal for you and your company.

Of course, first you have to understand how to do it.

How to Give Resale Permission:

Giving resale permission in and of itself is not difficult, but you want to make sure you do it the right way. Remember that you want to make it easy for your special report to get spread around. That means that you need to grant your resale permission the right way.

The best way to get started is with an opening statement that outlines your resale rights terms. Now, for some resale rights, you can offer up minimum resale prices, restricting free giveaways, and even restricting membership site usage.

However, if you are trying to spread a special report to build your business and your email list, then you should consider making your resale rights simple and easy to get.

The easier it is for someone to acquire the rights, the more likely they are to take on your report and start selling and giving it away. When you are trying to expand an email list, you need to make sure that you do add one resale right permission restriction. You need to make sure that the main text of your special report stays unchanged.

That will ensure that links and references to your website or company and thus assist you in growing your list. Overall Benefits of Granting Resale Permission For Your Special Report.

When you choose to offer resale permission on your special report, you can gain a number of advantages. For one, by granting resale permission, you are encouraging others to spread your report. That means more eyes reading the report and about your company.

Secondly, offering up resale permission gives you credibility. As other read the report and it is being resold, you become more of an authority on your subject and, by manner of extension, so does your company.

Finally, you create a viral situation. When you offer easy to get resale permission, you are basically enlisting a large number of people to spread your report one way or another. That just helps the word spread that much easier.

Email List Benefits of Giving Resale Permission:

What, though, does this all have to do with expanding your email list with qualified potential clients?

Simply, when you wrote your special report, you should have done so with proper wording and links so that your opt-ins would grow. With such links, references, and other referrals coming from your special report, you are looking for a way to get that report in front of as many potential clients as possible. So by granting resale permission, you are creating a way to get your report in front of more people.

The more people you have looking at the report, the more people you have getting the opportunity to look for more information with your company and the more likely you are to get people adding their names to your email list. This will help your email list to not only grow, but also to grow with qualified leads. As you can see, there is a lot to be gained by writing a special report and granting resale permission to others for it.

It is one of the most efficient strategies you can use to get your special report in front of as many people as possible. Remember to start with a report that actually has value.

In addition, make sure it directs people to your company website as well as your opt-in email list in order to build a better list of qualified potential clients.

Finally, give permission the right way. Do not overcomplicate things by putting a lot of restrictions on the resale rights. Instead, make it easy for people to acquire the resale permission and they will be more likely to take it.

Remember, you are trying to get your report to spread. You are not looking to make a profit on the report by itself.

So once you have that understanding, you can just allow people to spread your special report to all those potential clients and members of your email list.

Thus if you are looking for a way to spread your special report, check into the granting of resale permission.

You will be glad you did it.

Chapter 8: Using The Ad Swap

Whether you are writing an E-zine or building an email list, your clients are important. Have you already exhausted all other means of getting more email addresses? You may want to consider using Ad Swaps.

This is a way for you to not only to increase your client base, but also gain more revenue from other sources. You may find that something as small as swapping ad's with different companies will give you the boost you have been looking for.

So What Is "Ad Swapping"?

This is actually exactly what the name implies. You swap your firm's ad with another firm's ad. Finding an Ad Swap group is as simple as using your favorite search engine. There are many companies out there that are interested in Ad Swapping.

Swapping your ad with another company can greatly increase your chances of gaining more subscribers. When you swap ads with another company, you will be displaying their ad instead of your own.

This means that your ad must be short enough to work with the company's email layout, but also be informative enough to grab the attention of the reader in hopes to directing them to your website.

Ad Swapping is smart advertising. Many times when individuals are browsing the internet, they may not know what they are looking for, but those that are already subscribed to an E-zine or other list already know what they are looking for.

Using Ad Swaps Correctly:

By correctly choosing the right company to swap Ads with, you will greatly increase your use base. This is because the readers are already interested in what they are reading and see that the Ad pertains to what they are reading and also that it is recommended as a reputable site by the person who supplied the original email.

A simple Ad Swap can bring in double the amount of people that you have now.

Before you even consider swapping your Ad with another person, you need to create a one-line description that will really make readers want to click on your Ad.

The "Ad Headliner" is the single most important part of the Ad. Without it, you are not left with much. The Ad Headliner should not be very long but should contain enough information that grabs the reader's attention enough that they want to visit your Ad. This is the same as Internet Ads.

If there is a lot of text you must read before you figure out what they are trying to bring to you, you most likely won't click on it. For this reason, keep your Ad Headliner short and sweet but powerful.

Sometimes a few words will work best, its up to you to decide the right length that is informative without being long-winded. There are many different companies out there and it's important to make sure that the Ad you get in return will be fit for your client base, and vice versa.

One of the most important aspects to consider when you are looking to swap ads with any other person is how well their content relates to yours.

This just means that if your clients expect information about computer hardware, they aren't likely to click on an Ad that is about horse racing equipment.

This is not to say that everyone interested in computer hardware isn't interested in horse racing equipment, but at the time they are reading your E-zine, they may not really have that on their mind.

The topic of the Ad does not necessarily have to completely pertain to your Email, but it does need to be related. One other point to remember is to find out how many users the other person interested in the Ad Swap has.

Since you are interested in gaining new members, then it is in your interest to only swap Ad's with another person who currently has the same or more number of users. Of course, if you have only five percent more users than them, you can still give them a chance.

Just remember that you are interested in gaining new members, and if your Ad Swap partner has a fewer number of members, then your odds of gaining new members drops significantly.

What if you cannot find a company who shares the same interests to Ad Swap with? One solution to this problem might be creating a survey for your customers with a wide selection of topics for them to choose from.

This will help you understand what other interests they share, and can help you make a smarter decision on who to trade your Ad with.

back from all of your customers, you can safely choose one of the top interests and know that you will be doing your part in relaying traffic to your Ad Swap partner.

Choose your topics wisely though. You don't want to have your topics cover a gigantic area of interests, because finding a company that needs an Ad Swap partner with your particular interests may not want to trade with you if your material pertains to a topic that differs too greatly from the one they cover.

Offering your customers between Twenty to Thirty different interest topics to choose from will give them a nice selection, and make things easier when it comes time to find an Ad Swap partner. Joining an Ad Swap group can greatly increase the number of members you currently handle. It is one of the best ways to get more subscribers to your E-zine or other subscription email service. Be sure that you research each person who you are conducting the Ad Swap with as their content will be displaying to all of your subscribers and you are the one responsible if they supply you with a broken link. Be sure to write a few ad headliners and choose the one that is both minimalist and descriptive.

Without an attention-grabbing Headliner, an Ad Swap is useless. As long as you are sure to check over all of these points you should be on your way to conducting a successful Ad Swap.

Chapter 9: The Magic of Give-Away Events

Building an email list is one of the best ways to advertise the product or service that you are trying to market. This will keep your efforts focused on your target audience instead of to a broad range of people who may not need or want to do business with you.

For example, if your business deals with home improvement information and products, you would not likely appeal to someone who is living in an apartment.

The main purpose of building a large, active email list is to bring in a sizeable amount of active readers who are looking to you for good deals and benefits.

Successful e-zine creators often credit their good fortune with hosting Giveaways, or contests as incentive to get people to join. Of course, once they join they will expect to receive a well-composed and beneficial newsletter or else they will likely choose to unsubscribe.

A new business might not be able to afford to give away free products to subscribers in the beginning, especially without the knowledge of how successful the newsletter will be in bringing in actual profits.

This is why it is a good strategy to find at least one reliable affiliate who you can either trade products with, or that is willing to give you a wholesale price.

List Building Through Give-Away Events:

Before you approach anyone in search of partnership, you should be fully organized and have a sample newsletter ready to present to them.

Be confident and show them that you have the drive to put in the efforts that it will take to make it work. It may take patience and friendly persistence to have anyone agree to take on a risk involving finances.

However, this situation could be very beneficial for both parties. You will have the means to get a customer base built and, if they can supply you with their products to give away, they will build a good reputation and increase earning potential.

If you don't know where to begin looking for a business affiliate, try looking for a successful business of any size that is in the same product category. This could help you bring customers to each other.

You may not be comfortable asking for money or products, but you also have the option of trading equal parts of your products with theirs to give away to subscribers of your e-zine. They may choose to do the same, which would help both of you. Neither of the parties will lose much money considering low production cost to the manufacturer.

Using this strategy to bring in customers will have you making the money back in no time. A simple outline of what to do to find a partner is as follows: propose your strategy for building an e-zine newsletter to potential partners, show them a sample newsletter to gain their confidence, and use your skills of persuasion discuss ways that you could make the most of each of your products and help each other's business.

If they are hesitant and don't seem interested, move on. Anyone who has the ambition to start this type of venture will be able to find a partner who is just as eager to work with him or her.

Do NOT immediately advertise your Give Away.

It is important to wait until you receive the products that you will be sending out.

A formal contract should also be agreed upon and signed because they are a common practice in the business world. Decide when would be the best opportunity to give away a free product to subscribers.

If you do it at the time they sign-up you will risk having people sign up just for the gift and then canceling their subscription.

One way to ensure that your list grows, and remains active, is to require that membership is at least one month old before they can apply for the free gift.

Another alternative is to have a monthly drawing for the items you are giving away. That will keep readers of your e-zine entering each month for the contest.

This will give subscribers incentive and they may even help you by referring friends and family to join. Being aggressive in this situation will not hurt your reputation.

If you already have a great web site, don't hesitate to advertise the Give-Away exclusive to mailing list subscribers on every single page. It can be placed in a spot on the page that will not interrupt the flow of the page, such as the bottom or top corner.

Do you offer a site subscription?

Add a check box to the sign up page offering to automatically add them to the email list also. The free gift should not be the only reason they choose to sign up.

Offer a link to a sample of the newsletter so that potential customers can see the benefits and incentives that they will receive in each email.

You have to be ready to work hard to make people happy and keep them interested in what you have to offer. The double opt-in practice is important to anyone who is building a large mailing list. Anyone with genuine interest in becoming a part of your list will be willing to confirm their request to join twice.

This is your opportunity to remind them to add your address to their white list so that it is not filtered out with spam.

Using only single opt-in signups will bring in a large number but the quality of the list will definitely suffer.

You will either be filtered as spam or have to deal with a lot of un-subscribing from those who were never interested in what you have to offer.

Keep up the maintenance on your list.

Don't be afraid to ask for feedback from your active readers on what they would like to see more or less of.

This will let them know that you are genuinely interested in their business and satisfaction.

A Give-Away is a proven effective way to get a list started, but it is up to the creator to keep the list as active as it is large.

Chapter 10: Investing in Co-Registration Leads

Too often the key to your business working successfully is how much traffic you can drive to your website.

The type of product or services you offer can sometimes limit traffic.

This means not only do your potential sales suffer but so does the growth of your business. One way to improve this traffic flow is co-registration.

This means putting opt-in check boxes on the page where your customers register.

Co-Reg & Opt-Ins - They Go Hand-in-Hand:

Opt-in boxes are places that your customers, or even just those who visit your site, can check to say if they are willing to receive information on similar products, services or e-zine publications.

This allows you to build up an email list so that when you have sales or introduce new products you are able to get the word out to potential clients quickly.

Building mailing lists is an important part of running an online business. But, it is something you cannot necessary do all on own.

There are companies who can help you build mailing lists that will reach customers that will potentially be interested in what your site has to offer.

There are companies who will sell you co-registrations leads to help you build that all important mailing list. But before you agree to buy from them you must be certain that you will get exactly what you need. There are some basic guidelines to shopping around for a good co-registration service. To begin with, the company must guarantee you that the names you are being given are genuinely opt-in names.

The last thing you want to do when trying to bring in customers to view your offerings is to use names that have been collected without the customer's agreement and authorization. Then you also want them to guarantee you that the names have been generated recently.

Co-Reg Tips:

The age of the leads you invest in is a crucial factor. Names that were picked up a year ago will not likely be of any use.

People change their email addresses regularly when they change jobs or move. And, over time their interests change, as well. The products or services they were looking for which are common to your business may already have been bought.

That is what makes 'old' lists an even bigger waste of money.

The other thing to consider is price. The cost of co-registration lists varies from company to company so shop around until you find what you think is the best deal. Do not use price as the only factor, but use it as one of the factors. You want a company that will offer to you everything you need at a reasonable cost. Whether you are building your mailing list to draw people to your e-zine, announce new products or get new names for your monthly newsletter a service that offers you good co-registrations lists will save you time and a lot of work.

If you want a list that can bring you hundreds of names doing it yourself could take months. Getting them from a service cuts that to a matter of days and lets you get back to growing your business. There is no other lead generation resource better through the Internet than this.

If you are looking for a source of co-registration leads finding them on the Internet is not difficult. But you must try to find one that will offer you what you need.

The service at

https://smallbusiness.chron.com/coregistration-marketing-24798.html

seems to have a lot to offer to their potential clients, as do the folks over at List Opt. When checking out any list service, make sure that they offer is a guarantee that you will be satisfied with their products. Also be sure that they offer lists that are generated the correct way; with no contest lists being used to trick respondents into allowing their names to be taken. And it's VITAL that all their names are opting.

They will have co-registration lists that are aimed solely at that one area. This may be any form of product or service. One service that sells co-registration lists like this has them aimed particularly at those who are interested in Internet marketing. Their claim is that those who are on their lists are eager to find ways to make money on the net. So, if that is what you are offering on your website their co-registrations lists are for you. They can be found at Nitro List Builder. This particular company also offers larger lists than most others. They talk of the availability of lists that have from twenty to one hundred thousand contact names. Like the other one they promise their lists will be fresh ones.

Many of the co-registration sites that sell email leads are particular about what kind of businesses they will work with.

They will stay away from hot businesses, gambling sites or sites which reflect an attitude of hate against others. This shows that they are trying to make aim their business at others whose businesses do not hurt anyone.

They are careful to ensure that there will be no duplicate names and that all the leads you get are current. This is a very important aspect of co-registration leads and one that all services that sell these leads promise you.

You can always expect to get a few email addresses that have changed but if you wind up with too many dead leads you should contact the service you have bought from and demand replacements. If the number of dead leads is high they should honor your request. Some services will give you an extra one or two percent on your order to help ensure that you get the right number of goods leads for the money you have paid. Prices vary greatly on co-registration leads. You can pay anywhere from thirty-six dollars for one thousand names to three hundred dollars for twenty thousand names and many possibilities in between! You're Almost Finished With the guide Part Two... There you have it! Both the basics and advanced list building techniques are now as good as at your fingertips. Note though, that you require some substantial list and/or experience to use some of the advanced list building techniques discussed in this course, while others can be done just almost immediately. All in all, they can prove to be very powerful list builders if mastered correctly. It is my sincere wish that these techniques can help you expand your mailing list and in doing so, expand your Online Business Empire even further. See you at the top! (When you are ready for the "hardcore" level, let's get started with the guide Part Three... the last edition in the series... just scroll down!) Bringing Your Online Business To The Next Level Welcome to the last sequel in the Ultimate List Builder's Course series, where you will discover some of the most hardcore list building strategies as used and practiced by TOP Internet Marketers and gurus from around the planet! Now I am going to confess that it's not going to be necessarily easy to execute any one of these Master's Level of list building techniques, as they certainly require more practice backed by experience to leverage on them.

But it is a worthwhile learning journey as these list building techniques has been responsible for income breakthroughs of many an Internet Marketer, some who brought in thousands, potentially tens of thousands of red hot leads in a short time span, some literally overnight! I won't stall you any further as I could almost feel your excitement. Let's move on! Scroll down for chapter eleven... and learn more methods to help you build your list.

Chapter 11: Recruiting an Army of Affiliates

If you are an Internet marketer, one of the keys to a successful business will be your ability to bring potential customers to your website.

The best way to do this is to find a way to build large email lists of these potential customers. One of the most common strategies for doing this is purchasing opt-in co-registration lists.

An opt-in list, as you already know by now, are those where the customer has checked a box on a site saying that they are willing to receive information through their email for different products.

Building, or buying, these email lists are what will make the difference to a successful Internet marketing business. It does not matter what you are offering on your site, products you want to sell or services you are offering, if you do not have the traffic to your site you will not make money. IMPORTANT! You should not purchase lists that are not recently generated or that are not opt-in generated. If you do then you will not add to the success of your business but will find that too many of your leads are cold and you have spent money for very little, if any, benefit to your business.

Affiliate Programs Exposed:

Another way to drive traffic to your site is to become part of an affiliate program. This can be done either by joining an affiliate program that is already showing signs of success or by making one yourself.

Joining Affiliate Programs:

Joining an already established affiliate program has several benefits.

Obviously the first one is that the program is already up and running and so there is less work for you to do and less time to wait for results from the program. You would need to search the Internet and locate affiliate programs that are related to what your product or service is. It would make no sense to sign up to any program if the topic is not close to what you are doing. This does not mean that you should be concerned that you are signing up in a program that is run by your competition.

In reality any affiliate program you join that properly reflects what you are marketing on your website will have other members who potentially are your direct competitors.

This does not matter. Customers will shop around. If what you offer is a better product or service, with better financial considerations the customers will come to you.

This gets others to help increase your business prospects. What you want to do is get the affiliate programs to work for you. In this way you create your own email lists, use ones that you have bought and bring them all together through an affiliate site, which will not only generate potential customers for you but can potentially earn you money as you send customers to other sites.

With affiliate programs, if you join them, then you get commission on their sales. This can be a nice perk as you work to bring traffic to your site.

Creating Your Own Affiliate Program (RECOMMENDED!) If on the other hand it is your chose to create your own affiliate program you have the advantage of being able to have it exactly the way you want. Just remember as your affiliate site grows and is successful your will be paying commissions to others on your sales.

This is true of our own program or one you join. This practice is a reasonable one since what you are doing is attempting to get people to your site and the more methods you have that you can use the better. Think of it like having salespeople in your store. You would have to pay them a commission or salary to sell your goods. This is more or less the same thing.

With your affiliate site you will need to generate interest for the potential customer to come there and for others join. One way to do this is to have lots of interesting information for potential customers to read. These are usually in the form of articles.

These articles should be related to your product or service, but not all of them should be solely with the aim of selling. You will find that sometimes a less pressured sales pitch will attract more customers. Still you want to provide lots for them to read that is related to your Internet business.

Another way to bring people to your affiliate's site is make sure these articles have lots of keywords. Keywords are what the average person uses when they are searching for something on the net. For example, if a person is looking to buy a rattle for their friend's new baby, they will likely write in the words baby rattle, but they may also put in the words baby gift, new baby, baby toy etc. So, the more words that you can put in your articles that will come up in their search the more likely they will visit your site. You do not put the keywords in just once but several times so that your articles will come up nearer the top of a search. When creating your affiliates program you will want to have an interesting lead in for others to use. Pay per click is another option for you through your affiliates program. These can be highly successful but are often difficult to monitor. They can easily be abused by others to generate an income for themselves while not truly sending any traffic to your website.

Remember your affiliates program will generate your own email leads. As long as they are opt-in generated you also have the option of selling these lists. But most importantly you have them available to use along with any lists you have paid for to generate more traffic to your site as well as to help the customers who have joined your affiliate program. A common piece of advice to those who are trying to start up an affiliates program or just get an Internet business rolling is once you have discovered something that works, stay with it, then repeat it and continue your success!

Chapter 12: Leveraging on Joint Ventures

Electronic communications are the simplest way to sell your good or service today. As such, it only makes sense to continually expand your targeted email list.

But how do you go about doing this? One of the easiest ways is by networking with partners who also have email lists. However, if you are going to be effective with this, there are several things you have to keep in mind. Here are some tips on how to find partners with the tight type of email lists, and also how to use those lists to the mutual benefit of both parties.

Where To Look For Potential Partners One of the first places to check for potential partners is among professional associations. Often, you can build rapport very quickly with others who are in some way connected with the same general area of expertise that you offer with your service or product line.

Of course, you are not looking to partner with anyone who would be in direct competition with you and your company. But chances are the professional association membership will cast a wide enough net that you can find at least a few professional partners who are engaged in offering goods or services that are complimentary to what you have to offer.

As an example, let's say that you offer discounted international long distance services. You happen to belong to a professional organization for persons who are part of the telecommunications industry.

In addition to long distance, this would also include audio conferencing, web conferencing, and video conferencing. You might find it a very good fit to approach an audio conferencing provider about sharing qualified email listings. The potential for them to pick up some new conferencing customers is certainly there, and you may also find plenty of changes to snag some new corporate long distance clients as well. Along with professional associations that relate to your industry type, there are also the broader organizations, such as city and state chambers of commerce.

Membership in these types of organizations can easily pay for itself with just one good lead on someone to partner with. This will often involve making sure you attend chamber events, especially mixers.

The focus here is not necessarily to find persons who deal with services that are part of your industry, but persons whose clientele represent who new markets for you, and vice versa.

For instance, at a local chamber event, you strike up a conversation with a sales director for a national legal form supplier.

As part of their customer support, they have a monthly e-newsletter they send out to their clients. As it happens, you currently make your living selling transcription services, and have quite a few legal firms in your client base. While your two business interests may appear to not have much in common at first glance, there is plenty of reason for the two of you to talk.

You could certainly endorse the use of their forms supply business, and they in turn would be able to open doors for you to additional attorney firms, arbitration services, and others where transcriptions are key to the working day.

Trade magazines are also a great way to get leads on organizations that you may want to partner with and share email lists.

In order to do this effectively, you may want to look closely at the composition of your current client base. What industry types are represented in your base?

Which sectors of your client base are generating the most revenue for you on a monthly basis? Are there existing parts of your client base that you would like to grow?

Answers to these questions will help you determine which of the many different trade and industry magazines you want to subscribe to, and use as leads in securing venture partners.

Other Details in Joint Ventures Pay attention not only to the features, but also any columns that mention companies in passing. In like manner, see who is advertising in these magazines.

You may find some great leads among the ads. If there are classifieds in the back of the magazine, do not discount finding a good lead or two among those classifieds as well.

Of course, you do not want to forget online resources. Just about everyone is online these days in one form or another. Look for web sites that are dedicated to the type of good or service that you offer. Often, there will be links off those sites that can lead you to potential venture partners.

Many of these sites will have message boards that can also connect you with other persons who would be interested in sharing qualified email lists as part of a joint project. While these may take some time to cultivate, in the end they can provide a big payoff.

Don't forget the possibility of utilizing your own web site as a way to attract potential joint venture partners as well. Depending on your business model, it may be quite appropriate to create a page that is meant to attract potential partners in a join email sharing campaign. Provide some basic guidelines that have to be met, such as proof that the list is qualified, that it is a current and usable list, and that no one is included without express permission. Then provide a way for anyone interested to contact you about moving forward. It cannot be stressed enough that you make sure to only work with persons who can provide a legitimate email list of persons who have requested to receive email transmissions.

There are far too many email lists on sale these days that are antiquated or compiled from sources that would do nothing to help you reach your target audience.

Whether you meet a potential joint venture partner face to face at a chamber event, or make your first contact via a message board or a response to a query on your web site, you must set the standard.

Important JV Tip:

Make sure that you only deal with people who have the same level of ethics and respect for potential clients that you have worked long and hard to cultivate and establish.

Failure to do so will mean lost time and resources, few if any new clients, and most likely loss of some of your clients as well. Pick your partners carefully, however, and you will open up all sorts of opportunities to broaden your client base and increase your revenue stream.

Chapter 13: Executing Product Launches

As any good businessperson knows, nothing is quite as exciting as launching a new product or service. One of the best ways to have your new offering hit the ground running is by using a resource you already have in place to get the word out to interested parties: your customer email list.

Product Launch For Hard Hitters Utilization of your email list should begin long before the actual launch date of the new product or service. A savvy approach is to begin using the electronic communications to begin building up some interest in the new product.

As an example, let's assume that you do a monthly newsletter to your client list. Several months before the launch start inserting teasers into the newsletter.

Even something simple like "Not sure what to get your best friend for Christmas this year?

In September, we will tell you." Of course, you may want to be more direct and try something along the lines of "You told us you want it.

And we listened. Announcing Easy Web, our new web conferencing product, coming in August."

Of course, every month you will include a new tidbit about the new offering.

Use the space to extol the advantages of your offering over those from your competition.

Along with the teasers, build up to a feature article that goes into the background on how the product was developed and what influence existing customers had on the final design.

Customers love to know you listen, even if many of them never send you any ideas.

Pre-Launch:

As the time for the launch draws near, you may want to do some promotional work among your email listing as well. Offer premiums such as discounts to any existing client that can get someone who is not currently a customer to attend a demonstration of the product and who subsequently signs up for the product or service.

Among your client base, why not offer a short-term free trial, as well.

The point is to give your existing clients a chance to try your new offering, decide that they like it, and that they will be coming back for more.

Happy customers are some of the best word of mouth you will ever have, so if they like you and your new offering, they will be more than happy to promote you to other organizations.

In addition to using your regular e-newsletter to publicize the advent of your new offering, you may also want to do targeted emails from your email list.

Targeted emails would involve dividing your email list up according to industry type and preparing the text of an email that would point to applications of your new offering that are of special interest to that part of your client base.

As an example, you may have a large percentage of non-profit associations in your client base. You know that your new offering could help them keep track of participation in fund raising projects they conduct.

Focus on that point, explaining how your offering can make the job easier and more accurate.

Critical Launch Success Factors:

It is important to note that you will not get a very good response if you do not do two things. First, you must send several well-timed emails about your offering between the time you make the first announcement and the actual launch date. Far too many people think that one announcement does the trick and there is nothing more to be done.

The fact is the matter is that you want to use your email list to build interest for your offering as the launch date approaches. Depending on your client base, a monthly email might be just fine. If you think you can do so more often, than give it a try.

You want to keep people informed, give them ideas on how to use your offering, but you do not want them to get tired of seeing emails from you and decide to opt out of your list. Find that sweet spot for contacts and you will be able to use the list effectively.

Also, it is not a matter of using material versus sending out individual emails. By all means use both. Chances are that your clients will take note of one or the other, but not necessarily both forms of electronic communication.

Of course, you want the emails and the newsletter content to compliment one another.

In fact, you may want the text of your email to refer back to the content in the newsletter, and vice versa. Keep everything consistent and very upbeat.

Along with getting out information on the potential applications of your offering, you may want to invite your client base to participate in some sort of a contest, with the prize being something that would be useful in the home or office.

However you choose to construct the contest you need to make sure of two things. First, it is imperative that you be able to verify the results.

Secondly, you should offer a prize that will not create any undue hardship on your company. You want it to be attractive, but not something that will potentially create a situation where you would not be able to meet your obligations. Of course it makes sense to only offer a three-day, two-night cruise to the winner if you can afford to do so.

Launching Your Product:

Don't forget to follow up the launch date with some more updates and invitations to try out the new offering. Continue to spotlight the launched service or product in your e-newsletter and in email communiqués to your client for at least four to six months after the launch.

The potential for them to share your announcements and feature reports with other people will not end on the day of the launch. Keep the momentum going and you may pick up a few more customers.

Your email list is a valuable piece of property. It is important that you responsibly use it to keep your current customers happy with you and your offerings, as well as let them know of new innovations that can make life easier for them.

At the same, time, it can be a wonderful way to involve your clients in the process of securing new customers who can benefit from a working relationship with you. Make sure your customers always know how much you appreciate them and you will be able to not only maintain but also continue to expand your email list every time you have something new to offer.

Maximizing Your Mailing List Profit Points:

Having a solid mailing list is one of your business' greatest assets.

Many of us know that the single most powerful selling tool we have is the good word of mouth we get from our existing customers. The fact of the matter is that your customers can help you to grow your business in several ways, as you find ways to up-sell them on other means of helping you help them grow their business.

Here are some suggestions that will help you articulate to your customers how you can help them grow while you are maximizing the profits that you get from your mailing list and e-zines.

Sell Advertising Space To Your Clients:

Chances are that at least some of your clients are involved in selling goods and services that would be of interest to other customers on your mailing list. So what if you were to offer some really competitive advertising space in your monthly electronic magazine?

This one simple offer could begin a whole new revenue stream for you, using a resource that at present does not provide any direct profit. In order to keep things as simple as possible, you could specify the format of the ad and also offer sizes that would be very easy to include, such as quarter page, half page and page size advertisements. Just as with any ad service, you could offer short term and long term rates for advertising in the newsletter, which would mean a steady revenue stream for you over the long term. Along with the newsletter, have you thought about offering the contacts in your email list the ability to place ads with hot links on your web site? You could create a whole section of advertising that is just for your client base.

As for pricing, you could set up a basic monthly rate, and offer discounts off that for commitments of six months, a year, or two years of advertising via your web site.

Assuming that you send invoices through regular mail, you could also create a lucrative revenue stream by advertising to contacts on your email list the ability to include advertising flyers in all your mailings.

Of course, you would want to pieces to fit nicely into standard business envelope and you would want to make sure you kept the number of inserts to a minimum. Nevertheless, you could create a steady flow of cash from even this type of endeavor.

Another form of advertising you could offer to your clientele is to include a onetime feature article in your monthly E-zine.

The article could include an overview of the history of the company, vital information about their core product line, or information about an upcoming new good or service they will be launching soon.

This feature article option could be offered with a guaranteed minimum word count as well as a bold header, for a flat rate price. Of course, you could also offer a sliding scale based on a fixed rate per word instead of the flat fee. This would allow your client to opt for a longer article, if they wish to do so.

Affiliate Programs And Your Email List:

The simple fact of the matter is that no one is successful with an affiliate program without owning a good solid email list. Since you already have a list that meets those qualifications, why not put your email list to work and make some money with affiliate programs?

Here Is What You Need To Do:

The genius of opting into an affiliate program is that you get to expand the types of goods and services that you offer to your existing customer base without having to invest anything into development, facilities, or production.

Someone else has already done all of that. By entering into an affiliate agreement, you tap into that resource, act at the mediator, and rake in profit off every unit sold.

One of the first things you will need to do is collect data on available affiliate programs. A quick Internet search will probably lead you to quite a number of potential programs that would be of interest to you.

You may also uncover a source or two that will provide you with quick overviews of hundreds of affiliate programs that are actively looking for persons just like you.

Make notes of anything and everything that you think could possibly be of interest to you. One thing to note here is that you will be able to find plenty of affiliate programs that will work just fine with your own sense of business ethics.

While there may be some programs out there that offer products that you would prefer to not be connected with, do not worry about limiting yourself. The breadth and depth of affiliate programs is such that you will have no problem finding plenty to chose from. After you have made your initial swing through the lists, is it time to begin matching up your interests and skill sets with what you understand about your own clientele.

As you look at each of the affiliate programs that have caught your eye, think in terms of what your customers do for a living. What products or services would be likely to compliment what you already sell, or at least be of some interest to those that already know and do business with you?

You can sign up for all sorts of affiliate programs, but if they are not going to excite those who already know you, then what is the point? Make sure that any affiliate program you sign up with has the potential to generate additional income from your email list.

Next, you want to do some checking on any affiliate program that you are sure is a good fit for you and the customers on your existing email list. What will you be looking for?

Find evidence that the program is stable, that it delivers what it promises, and that the majority of the folks who are affiliates are happy with the way things are going. Where will you find this information? On the Internet, of course.

Use your Internet browser to conduct a search for comments on the affiliate program of your choice. You want to locate as much feedback, both positive and negative, as you can manage.

No organization is going to be without its detractors, so don't let some negative comments turn you off immediately. How well an organization responds to the need to resolve an issue with an unhappy client says as much about it as having customers who do not experience problems.

What you do want to be aware of are any trends that indicate the affiliate program is misleading in some way, that it fails to live up to its promises, and that it consistently has a history of leaving affiliates in the lurch.

When you find ample evidence of that sort of behavior, then you know it is time to forget about that program and move on to the next one on your list.

Once you have identified one or more affiliate programs that you feel good about representing, then the next move is to let the folks on your email list know what is going on. Prepare a press release announcing your decision to open a working relationship with your new partner.

Outline some of the reasons why you have decided that these affiliates are a good match for what you already provide to your customers. You may want to include some bullets that demonstrate some reasons why your customers should look at your new partner(s) very closely.

Make sure that you have a link set up on your web site that will function as a portal to your new partner(s), so you can get credit for any business your clients do with any of your partners is credited to you.

If you have an E-zine that you produce on a regular basis, promote the products of your partners right along with your own services.

Keep the name of your affiliate partner(s) in front of your customers through the use of both email and your E-zine, as well as making sure there is a link to your partner on your web site.

Along with opening up new revenue streams by using your email list to promote this new affiliate relationship, you also can make sure that your existing customers have the means to pass on your information to their associates.

This can lead to the expansion of your opt-in email listing, additional demand for your own services, and increase revenue from your affiliate relationship as well.

Always Remember To Market Your Own Services One of the reasons you have such a great email list in the first place is that people have come to know you and trust you.

You've sold them goods and services before, and they have liked what they got both in the way of product and in the way of customer care.

Your job is to not only maintain that positive relationship, but also to build upon it. Upselling is the term that is normally used for the process of promoting goods and services to your existing clientele that they have not yet tried out. In many ways, this is much easier than trying to start with a new lead. There is already a history between you and the buyer, one that has demonstrated a good working relationship up to that point.

Chances are that your client will at least devote a few minutes to whatever new product or service that you want to introduce them to. It is your job to use the resources at hand to make sure that courtesy of giving you a few moments turns into a sale.

When it comes to email announcements, make them big and broad, but keep in mind that not all people utilize HTML setting for their inbound email.

For that reason, you may want to rely more heavily on the content and less of using graphics to spotlight a new or existing service.

In order to get the most our of your email announcement content, you will want to observe a few basic rules. First, make sure that the content of the email announcement is focused. Do not try to cover too much ground at one time.

Keep the content in line with the purpose of the email, which is to promote one particular product in your line.

If availability is pending, make that clear right up front, including the date that the product will be available. Outline at least three possible applications of the product that, based on your knowledge of your customer base, will appeal to a majority of them. Close with contact information to learn more about the product, including a link back to the page on your web site that features the product.

Second, make your email announcement can be easily scanned by your audience. Many people will glance over your email and then move on.

You can diminish that occurrence by having the announcement broken down so that key points will catch the eye of even the most casual reader and impel him or her to go back to the beginning and read all the way through.

Using headers and bullets are an effective way to make your announcement more scanner friendly, and will help hold the attention of the reader.

Last, make sure the email announcement is simply that: an announcement. The communication is not meant to function as a sales brochure, nor is it supposed to be an exhaustive study of the new product. It is meant to spark the interest of the reader and provide them with just enough detail to compel them to want more information. Generally speaking, if you can keep the announcement under 500 words, you will manage to keep the attention of your audience long enough to make your point.

In Conclusion... As the last section of the series in the Ultimate List Builders Course draws to an end, remember: your email listing can help you to generate additional AND substantial ongoing revenue for your Online Business. By offering advertising space on your web site and in your E-zine, you provide customers with the chance to reach a whole new audience, one that already trusts you to steer them in the right direction.

The use of affiliate programs creates opportunities to build on the relationships you already have with everyone who has opted into receiving electronic communications from you by offering them a wider range of products and services. Last, your email list provides you with a bank of persons who are already receptive to doing business with you, and will often be very happy to know about any new goods or services you are offering to them. With each of these three examples, and especially if you allow them to overlap in the way you utilize your email list, you have the opportunity to greatly expand your revenue stream, as well as broaden your client base.

To Your Ultimate Mastery Of List Building & The Maximizing Of Your Profits!

To Your Complete Success!

Resources:

Besides the links throughout the course, there are a few other favorite resources I'd like to share with you. I've used them myself and so I can confidently recommend them to you for your business.

Marketing & Business Tools You'll Need:

Payment Processor:
2CheckOut is my favorite

Clickbank is only for digital products but is good, too PayPal is a good free alternative to get started out Hosting:

HostGator is a place for hosting multiple domains very affordably.

Domain Name Registrar:

Ifastnet.com offers excellent service & pricing plus some other extras you may need besides your domain names.

Autoresponders:

All of these are good solid (and necessary) products...

AWeber

GetResponse

ListMailPro

FollowUpExpert:

MyAutoresponderPro

My Favorite List-Building Resources:

Click Funnels

Nitro List Builder

List-Opt's List Builder

Awesome Membership Site Script:

Amember works great for an affordable, easy member site script!

How To Use Creative Marketing To Sell Your Products And Services !

This Book Will Teach You How To Get More Clients

And Grow Your Business !

This Is Fifth Bonus Book !

By : "Santiago Johnson Smith"

TABLE OF CONTENTS – 5° Bonus Book

How To Creative Marketing To Sell Your Products And Services !

Chapter 4 – Creative Marketing Methods

Word of Mouth

What is it?

How do you do it?

Summary

Canvassing

What is it?

How do you do it?

Summary

The Sign Says

What is it?

How do you do it?

Summary

Vehicle and Body Advertising

What is it?

How do you do it?

Summary

Promotional Items

What is it?

How do you do it?

Summary

Chapter 5 – Digital Creative Marketing

Establishing yourself

Website basics

Internet marketing basics

Going Viral

What is it?

How do you do it?

Summary

Beating the Blog Drum

What is it?

How do you do it?

Summary

Chapter 6 – Rules and Regulations

Fairness in Advertising

What It Means

Spam Isn't Healthy

Weird Laws and Ordinances

Chapter 7 – Welcome to the Jungle

Table of Figures

Chapter 1 – How and Why Creative Marketing Works

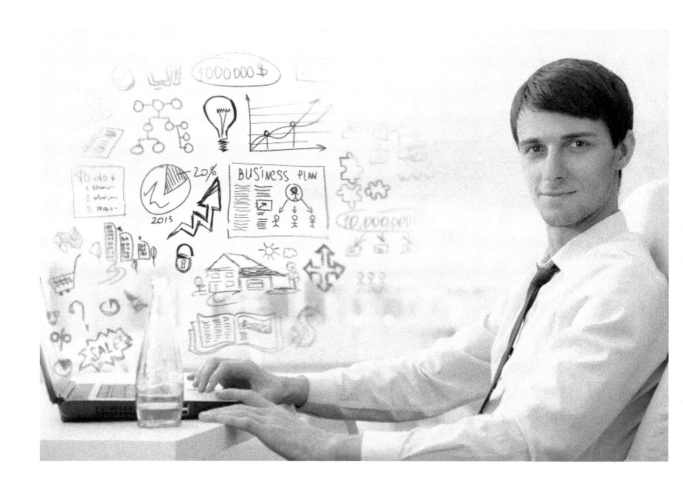

Today's business market is an extremely competitive place. More businesses enter the fray all the time: for the past ten years, more than 750,000 new startups spring into existence across North America. Unfortunately, over 60 percent of new businesses fail in the first four years.

Why do they fail? According to a study performed by the U.S. Department of

Commerce, there are three main reasons startup businesses fold:

Lack of financial planning Poor sales skills

Poorly planned and executed marketing

Creative marketing addresses all three of these concerns. It is one of the most successful marketing methods available, and since it is low-cost and high-impact, you won't need a huge advertising budget to take advantage of this powerful strategy.

What you will need is a basic understanding of how and why Creative marketing works.

The Element of Surprise

One of the reasons Creative marketing works is that the methods are often unexpected. Many Creative campaigns are highly visible, and contain some sort of element that is unique to the business using it.

Though it is something of a cliché by now, you should be prepared to "think outside the box" when it comes to planning your Creative marketing campaign. The classic, expensive methods of advertising your business should be employed sparingly, if at all. These include:

Yellow page advertisements

Newspaper or magazine advertisements Radio or television commercials

Think about it: when is the last time you were heavily influenced by a yellow page, newspaper, magazine, radio, or television advertisement? The fact is that today's consumers are so bombarded with advertising messages, they've learned to tune out the traditional sources.

As a Creative marketer, your goal is to catch them off-guard, and advertise in unexpected places. Many times, consumers won't even recognize your marketing efforts as advertising.

The good news is: you can usually do this for a fraction of the cost of traditional advertising venues. Creative marketing trades effort for money. You will work harder on your marketing than a mega-corporation with a million-dollar ad budget, but if you are persistent and creative in your efforts, they will pay off.

It Pays to Be Different

Remember the old Arby's slogan: "Different is Good"? This catchy little phrase could serve as a basic premise for one of the primary reasons Creative marketing tactics are so successful.

You might have a product or service that is completely unique. However, the chances are greater that you're competing with dozens or hundreds of other businesses for the same market share. One of the strengths of Creative marketing is the ability to capitalize on the aspect or aspects of your business that make you different -- and therefore worthy enough for consumers to spend their hard-earned money on your product or service.

So, what's different about your business? Here is a brief list of possibilities to investigate. Your business might offer:

The best, friendliest, or most attentive customer service. The lowest prices. Products that are higher quality than the competition.

A wider range of products than other businesses in your area or field. The simplest ordering methods.

Fast, convenient, and/or reliable delivery.

More expertise in your area than your competition.

The most informative and easiest to navigate website.

This aspect of your business is sometimes referred to as your USP, or Unique Selling Proposition. Once you have determined your USP, you know what makes your business different -- and different is good!

Controls and Variables

As with any marketing campaign, there are a lot of different variables that concern the outcome of your Creative marketing efforts. Some have to do with your business, which is often largely in your control. Others have to do with your customers, which are not always under your control.

When it comes to your business, the variables you will have to consider during the planning stage of your marketing campaign include:

Your location: If you run a brick-and-mortar business, where will your customers come from? Is there a decent amount of walk-in traffic, or are you situated out of the way? If you work from home or online, is your website at a good "location" - meaning well ranked with search engines, and parked at a domain that is easy for people to remember or stumble across?

Your product or service: The specific tangible and intangible items offered by your business will play a large role in determining how you'll market yourself.

Your target market: What is the best way to reach people who are most likely to become your customers? Identifying and reaching your target market is covered more extensively in chapter 3 of this book.

Your attitude: Though this is not an aspect that is specific to your business, it is one that you can control. If you remain positive and upbeat in your approach to business, your marketing efforts will reflect that attitude -- and your customers will notice.

What about your customers? Other people's reactions are for the most part beyond your control. You may have the best sales pitch and the most compelling marketing campaign out there, but potential customers who happen to be having a bad day when they see your message aren't likely to react in your favor.

However, there are some things you can control in regard to your customers. One of these things is to understand why people buy -- what brings them from initial interest to final sale. There are many different reasons, so you should determine which of them might apply to your business and focus on them.

To name just a few, consumers buy products or services that will:

Make them money (turnkey or reseller programs are a good example of this). Get them praise (gifts, new clothing).

Keep up with the Joneses (when "everyone else" has something). Make them look younger, better, or smarter.

Possess beautiful objects or works of art. Make them more comfortable.

Be more efficient, either at work or at home. Make their work easier or faster.

Help them avoid hard work.

Protect their family or their possessions. Excite or entertain them.

Inform them or enrich their lives. Allow them to escape stress.

Boost their popularity or reputation. Save them money or time.

Help them express emotions to others. Satisfy their curiosity.

Attract the opposite sex.

Help them avoid missing an opportunity.

It is important to become familiar with the needs your business fulfills for your customers. Armed with this knowledge, you can build a marketing campaign that points out the benefits consumers will realize when they purchase your product or service.

Fun with Case Studies

Does Creative marketing really work? Since the widespread embrace of the concept, many companies have undertaken successful Creative marketing campaigns. Innovation is often the key to a thriving business, and the following companies are examples of Creative effectiveness in action.

Several Campaigns That Worked

Saint Paul, Minnesota: Before the opening of the first Crazy Carrot Juice Bar, marketer Eric Strauss engaged in some forward thinking. He spent $73 to put together a life-sized carrot costume, which was worn at several special events around town. Over the next year, the "Carrot" made many public appearances. It was featured in various print, radio, and television media, and became largely responsible for catapulting the company's success. Eventually, the Crazy Carrot Juice Bar expanded to five stores and 65 employees, and was then sold to industry giant Jamba Juice -- all for a mere $73 investment.

Irvington, New York: The Flying Fingers Yarn Shop, just outside of Manhattan, was looking to expand its customer base. At the suggestion of a marketing consultant, the company secured three giant balls of yarn, complete with knitting needles, to the roof of a modified van and called it the Yarn Bus.

On weekends, the Yarn Bus travels between Irvington and NYC, promoting visibility and making special appearances at news events. Flying Fingers has seen a good increase in store traffic, but more importantly, people who might not make the physical trip to the store are made aware of their website, where they can learn about knitting classes offered by the store and purchase knitting supplies. The high visibility of the Yarn Bus has produced excellent results.

Manhattan, New York: Even not-for-profit businesses look to expand their reach. The Marble Church sought a way to attract younger members and revitalize their congregation. So, they turned to a marketing firm who came up with some unusual ways to get the word out.

One Labor Day weekend, hundreds of weekend visitors to the Hamptons spotted an airplane banner bearing the intriguing message: "Make a friend in a very high place.

Marblechurch.org." In addition, the church rented a low-cost mobile billboard (mounted on the side of a van) that drove around Manhattan. The sign read: "In This Town It Doesn't Hurt to Have God on Your Side."

These creative messages, delivered in creative ways, introduced Marble Church to people who would otherwise never have heard of the place. As a result, the church reported a 31% increase in membership.

Oregon: Odd giveaways abound. People are intrigued by the unusual, which may explain why the Les Schwab tire dealership's "free beef in February" promotion keeps customers coming back, or why a nearby bank receives excellent local media coverage for their yearly tradition of giving away free Vidalia onions to anyone who walks in.

One Campaign That Didn't

Remember the backfiring efforts mentioned in the first chapter?

Recently, a Creative marketing campaign took a surprisingly bad turn in Boston, Massachusetts. In an effort to promote a new animated television series, Aqua Teen Hunger Force, the Cartoon Network designed and installed 40 magnetic light displays depicting characters from the series, and mounted them in various locations in and around Boston.

Unfortunately, Boston citizens reacted with suspicion to the devices, which included batteries and wires hooked to the back of the placards to control the lights. Reports of the signs caused a city-wide panic in post-9/11 fashion, and "an army of emergency vehicles" responded to the situation. Several bridges, subway stations and highways were closed while police examined and in some cases destroyed the signs.

What marketing impact did this incident have for Cartoon Network? It certainly raised awareness of the program, but when it comes to your business, you may not want this level of advertising. TV columnist David Hiltbrand stated for the Philadelphia Inquirer: "Those wacky marketing guys at Turner Broadcasting. Because, let's face it, nothing says cartoon hijinks quite like a red-level terrorist threat."

Chapter 2 – Creative Marketing for Your Small Business

In this chapter, we'll start with a closer look at what Creative marketing entails, and then discuss some of the groundwork you should be doing before you plan and execute your campaign.

Unlike other marketing methods, which rely on a huge influx of cash and resources designed to bring about immediate results, Creative marketing takes time and continual effort to sustain. In any marketing venture, it can be difficult to gauge the effectiveness of a particular technique. When it comes to Creative marketing, you will notice results that are a culmination of many different areas.

Let me introduce you to Jay Conrad Levinson. According to the father of the intense 'out of the box' Guerrilla marketing, the following basic principles lie at the heart of the Creative world:

Though large corporations have used Jay's Guerrilla techniques with some success, the methods are best geared for small businesses.

Creative marketing is based on principles of human psychology -- the study of the various ways consumers react to a marketing message -- rather than experience and guesswork.

A combination of marketing methods is a must for Creative success -- do not rely on a single advertising venue

Embracing current technology is of primary importance. Creative marketing is all about the cutting edge.

You should plan to invest significant portions of time, energy, and creativity into your Creative marketing strategy, rather than money.

Instead of sales volume, your business success should be measured in profits. Creative marketing campaigns concentrate on building new relationships with

complementary businesses, rather than trying to beat out the competition.

Shift your focus away from getting new customers; instead, aim for more, larger transactions with existing customers and more customer referrals (facilitating word of mouth, which is discussed in the next chapter).

Is Creative marketing right for your business? In most cases, the answer is yes.

Advantages

We'll start with the good stuff:

Creative marketing is cheap. At the high end, you may end up investing a few hundred dollars in promotional items or a major, centralized piece that you can build a number of different campaigns around (such as the carrot suit in the examples listed in chapter 2). At the low end, it's free -- and you can't beat free!

In addition to growing your business, Creative marketing involves networking, both with your customers and with other businesses. In the process of executing and maintaining your campaign, you will make a lot of new friends and allies.

Creative marketing is specifically tailored to meet the needs of small businesses, whereas traditional advertising venues are complicated and expensive to the point of exclusion (bordering on snobbishness).

Many aspects of Creative marketing campaigns are just plain fun! You get to perform wacky stunts and engage in unusual activities, all in the name of working for a living.

Creative marketing works. If you do your research, plan your campaign, and stick with it, you will more than likely end up with a better and more profitable business.

Disadvantages

And now, the bad:

Creative marketing works -- but it is not completely failsafe. It is, after all, advertising; which is far from an exact science. The number of variables involved in advertising guarantees that nothing is 100 percent effective.

As with any advertising campaign, you will not be able to pinpoint exactly what works and what doesn't. Obtaining measurable results is difficult (but not impossible, unlike other marketing techniques).

Creative marketing requires a greater level of dedication and energy than traditional advertising venues, which often consist of throwing large amounts of money at other people to do the work for you.

If you're looking for a quick fix, Creative marketing is not your solution. You will not see instant or overnight results stemming from your efforts. An investment of time is required in order to achieve your business sales goals.

Creative marketing is not for the thin-skinned or faint of heart. At the very least, you will have a few detractors who find fault in your methods. At worst, you may be threatened with legal action (which is why it's so important to check your local laws before engaging in a Creative marketing campaign).

Cost Breakdown: Money versus Effort

What is worth more: your money, or your time?

This is the trade-off involved in Creative marketing. You don't need a lot of money, but if you don't invest your time, your efforts will not pay off. The principles behind Creative marketing (listed in the beginning of this chapter) require planning, groundwork, and effort.

How can you tell whether it's worth the trade-off?

Here is a brief, hypothetical example.

One popular marketing method is to send out e-mail announcements in the form of a regular weekly or monthly newsletter. You could build a mailing list and create your own newsletter (the Creative method) or you could buy advertising space in another business's newsletter (the traditional method).

If you choose to advertise in another newsletter:

You will spend somewhere between $100 and $1000 for premium space in a widely read newsletter (e-zine) with a big subscriber list. You may end up spending more for consecutive ads, since consumers typically need to see your message 3 to 7 times before they'll buy.

You will spend a few to several hours researching e-zines, writing your advertisements or article, and contacting the e-zine owners in order to schedule your ad's appearances.

You will typically see a conversion rate (number of people who read your advertisement compared to number of people who become your customers) of 2 to 5 percent - slightly higher than the conversion rate of a direct mail campaign. This rate typically goes up a few percentages with subsequent advertisements, depending on the effectiveness of your copy (the wording of your message).

If you create your own newsletter or e-zine:

You will spend $0 to $100 (you may decide to invest in desktop publishing software, list management software or services, or an upgraded Internet service provider plan to handle additional web traffic).

You will spend several hours to several months building your opt-in subscription base, through methods like sign-up boxes, refer-a-friend programs, e-zine directory listings, and word of mouth. You will realize the typical conversion rate at first (2 to 5 percent) - but you will never

have to spend another penny for advertising, because you own the newsletter or e-zine. Your subscription base will continue to grow, and your sales resulting from your

newsletter will increase exponentially, rather than in the measured bursts you can expect from the "traditional" method.

One thing to be wary of when you're building an e-zine subscription base is buying bulk lists and using "free traffic" programs to bulk up your subscribers. Though this will give you some impressive numbers, the majority of these will either delete your e-mails unread, or unsubscribe as soon as they've met the requirements of whatever benefit they signed up for. The best results will come from a carefully targeted subscriber list that you have built yourself.

Determining your money-versus-time factor

How can you figure out whether the time you'll invest in a given Creative marketing campaign is worth the trade-off in advertising dollars -- assuming, of course, that you have a substantial advertising budget to begin with? (If you don't, no worries; you don't need one!)

You can get a rough estimate of your results by performing the following steps:

1.   Determine a traditional advertising venue that most closely relates to your intended Creative marketing effort.

2.   Estimate the total monetary cost of each method.

3.   Estimate the total time investment involved with each method.

4.   Assign a reasonable dollar value to each hour of your time you would invest ($15 an hour is a good average).

5.   Add monetary costs and per-hour time costs to each method, arriving at two separate totals.

6.   Calculate a projected profit resulting from each of the methods (don't forget to factor in the "snowball" effect gained from Creative marketing through repeat business and customer referrals - most traditional advertising venues are one-shot deals).

7.   Subtract total cost from total profit.

This will give you a general idea. Usually, the Creative marketing campaign will end up looking like a much better deal.

Finding Your Target Market

Before you attempt to sell your products or services, you need to know to whom you're selling them. Market research is an important step in any advertising campaign, and one that is unfortunately overlooked too often. Without a good handle on your target market, you will be wasting your time, effort and money.

The most effective marketing is designed to specifically reach the people who are most likely to buy your product or service. This is one reason why traditional advertising has such a low response rate. Just about everyone has access to television, radio, and print media like newspapers and phone books. Only a small percentage of those people will be in your target demographic.

There are two steps to target marketing, which is also referred to as niche marketing. The first is to define your target, and the second is to find ways to reach them. Once you have accomplished these steps, you can incorporate this information into a Creative marketing campaign that will give you the most bang for your buck (or more likely, your efforts).

Identifying your niche

This step involves a close analysis of your business. Much like an investigative reporter, you need to determine the who, what, where, when, and why of your customer base. Ask yourself the following questions:

Would your product or service appeal more to men, women, or both genders equally?

What age range does your product or service appeal to? (Note: if your business sells products or services for children, parents are your target demographic).

What is the range of income and education level of the people who may be interested in your product or service?

Are they single? Married? With children? Retired?

How will your customers use your products or services? Is there a potential for repeat business?

Does your product or service fall into the category of needs (food, clothing, shelter) or wants (luxury items)?

What makes your product or service unique (your USP -- discussed in Chapter 2)? Is your product an impulse buy (books, shoes, gourmet food) or an investment (cars, boats, computer hardware or software)?

How are transactions for your product or service typically carried out -- online, mail order, or in person? Cash, check, or credit cards? A single payment, multiple payments, or monthly recurring fees?

How do your potential customers typically become alerted to new products or services? Online, through public advertisements, from the news media, or some other method?

You may even want to develop a profile of your ideal customer (for example, 20-30 year old single college-educated females, or 40-50 year old married males with middle-class incomes) to help you pinpoint your target market.

Locating your niche

Once you have determined what type of customer you're looking for, you have to find where they hang out. Do they frequently eat at restaurants or go to movies? Would they be more likely to spend an afternoon at a shopping mall or a library? Are they frequent travelers, and would you be able to reach them at airports and bus or train terminals?

For online marketing, you can often find specific forums for your target demographic. Keep in mind that when you're marketing online, you have to build a rapport with online communities before you can start pitching your business. After all, you wouldn't walk into a complete stranger's house and shove your products in their faces demanding a purchase, would you? This may sound like an extreme example, but when it comes to Internet protocol, this is exactly what people seem like when they drop into forums and immediately start posting advertisements and special deals.

Use the information you find about your target customers' buying habits to determine the best ways to focus your Creative marketing efforts. If your customers like to eat out, consider striking an exchange with a local restaurant. If they travel, think about bus billboards or materials you can hand out in terminals.

Chapter 3 – Creative Marketing Methods

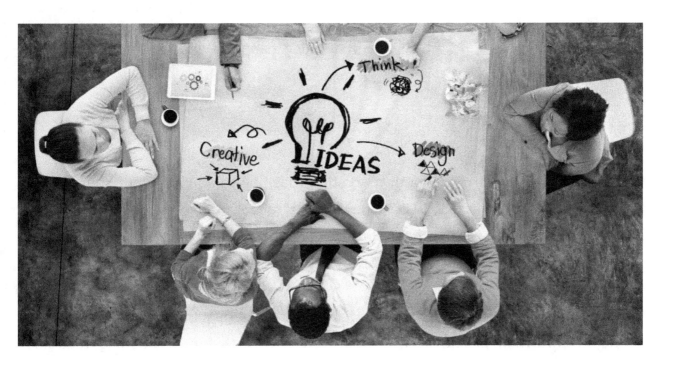

Now that you know what Creative marketing can do for your business, it's time to learn how to do it! In this chapter, we'll explore some of the methods you can use to build buzz and grab your customers' interest.

Keep in mind that there are many different approaches to Creative marketing, and your strategy should include some elements that are unique to your business. You don't have to follow these methods to the letter -- in fact, experimentation is a great way to hit on that perfect marketing strategy that will deliver the gold for you. Feel free to tweak these methods and create an approach that is uniquely yours.

Word of Mouth

Word of mouth marketing is arguably the most powerful and effective strategy out there. Unfortunately, it is also the most elusive and difficult to control.

This marketing method relies more on your customers than on your efforts, and can usually be traced to the quality of your product or service.

To put it another way: word of mouth marketing happens when a product or service "sells itself."

What is it?

People like to talk. Word of mouth marketing, basically, is giving them something to talk about: your business. It is building a "buzz" about your product or service, and letting your customers do the marketing legwork for you by telling friends, family, and sometimes even complete strangers if they're excited enough.

Word of mouth marketing is powerful, because it is genuine. You can't fake this phenomenon. When people believe what you have is worth mentioning to others, they're going to be enthusiastic -- and that enthusiasm helps to generate even more business for you in the form of new customers and wider market recognition.

There are many different forms word of mouth marketing can take. Just a few of them are:

Viral marketing: Crafting and distributing a high-impact message that it easy to pass along to others—often through e-mail (viral marketing will be discussed further in Chapter 5).

Community marketing: Joining or forming a shared-interest community whose members are likely to enjoy your product or service. Note that with community marketing, it is important to place the good of the community first, and marketing efforts last. Marketing will evolve naturally through participation.

Buzz marketing: Creating an air of excitement or mystery around your business, usually through news, entertainment, or underground campaigns.

Grassroots marketing: Coordinating groups of volunteers to spread your message on a personal or local level.

Cause marketing: Dedicating part of your business to a social cause, which in turn earns respect and support from others dedicated to the same cause.

Conversion creation: Catch phrases, promotions, launch parties, and other memorable tools or events designed to spread through word of mouth.

Product seeding: Identifying influential or key individuals and getting your product or information into the right hands at the right time.

How do you do it?

As previously stated, even though word of mouth is effective, it's hard to pull off. If you try to fake a buzz for your business, consumers will smell a scam and your efforts will backfire.

There are, however, a few things you can do to help encourage word of mouth advertising to start on its own.

1.   Have a quality product or service. This may sound too obvious to consider, but it is perhaps the most important factor in word of mouth marketing. Make sure your customers are getting what they pay for. Research the competition -- you're going to want to know if several other businesses are offering comparable products or services at far lower (or higher) prices than you. If possible, back your product or service with a guarantee or warrantee.

2. Put your customers first. A happy customer is one who feels their purchases are important to your business. Happy customers are potential word of mouth marketing sources. Make delivering on your promises a top priority. If you offer fast shipping, be certain your products are always delivered in a reliable and timely manner. If your service promises quick turnaround, make sure you never miss a deadline. Address customer complaints and problems immediately and personally, and consider offering refunds or bonuses for dissatisfied customers.

3. Identify and speak to your target market. Who is interested in your products or services? Where do they tend to gather -- either on or off-line? Blanket advertising is ineffective at best. Your marketing efforts should be concentrated on those venues or locations where your target consumer group is most likely to see your message. Once you create a community buzz among people whose shared interests lead them to your business, your marketing campaign becomes self-supporting.

4. Make it easy for your customers to tell others about your business. Word of mouth marketing is based on spreading your message. However, if interested customers don't have a way to share their enthusiasm with others right away, they may not remember what excited them about your product or service. Provide your face-to-face customers with business cards, flyers, or an accessible sign-up list for your company newsletter (you do have a newsletter, don't you?). Online, tools such as forums and refer-a-friend programs will help to facilitate spreading the word.

5. Listen and respond. If you receive a single complaint, you can often deal with it on a personal, individual basis. However, if you receive several similar complaints, you may need to do more than simply reply to the dissatisfied customers. Be prepared to make changes in your business according to the wants and needs of your customers. This applies to positive suggestions as well as complaints.

Also, if you discover that your business is being slammed, don't be afraid to defend yourself in a logical, reasonable manner (avoid flame wars). Customers respect businesses that are willing to admit their mistakes and will try to repair the damage.

Summary

Word of mouth marketing happens when a product or service "sells itself" through the enthusiasm of the consumer

Word of mouth marketing cannot be faked; it stems from genuine compassion on the part of both business and customer

There are many different forms word of mouth marketing can take

Word of mouth marketing cannot be engineered, but it can be encouraged The customer is the most important factor in word of mouth marketing

Word of mouth marketing is one of the least expensive and most powerful forms of Creative marketing

Canvassing

You may have seen this term used in conjunction with political campaigns, and in fact that's one of the most common reasons to employ canvassing. However, this technique can also be used effectively for Creative marketing.

What is it?

Canvassing refers to advertising that reaches out to a group of target consumers, usually in the same geographic location, on an individual level.

A simple example of a canvassing campaign would be a new pizza place sending its employees out with stacks of flyers, to be left on or under as many doors in their delivery area as possible.

Other canvassing techniques include:
Door to door introductions (think Jehovah's Witness here). Parking lot flyer distribution.

Sidewalk or mall sampling. Telephone campaigns.

How do you do it?

Though there is some monetary expense involved in most canvassing campaigns (usually to print the materials you plan to distribute), this type of marketing can be both inexpensive and effective. There are three stages to a successful canvassing campaign: planning, preparation, and distribution.

Planning: This, of course, is the most important. You have to plan the materials themselves, and you also have to determine the distribution area or method that will be most effective for you and your business.

For a local business, you will of course be interested in canvassing locally. You can distribute flyers door to door (be sure to check your area laws before you start passing out material this way), hang them on community bulletin boards or telephone poles (again, check with local ordinances here), or plan an area mailing campaign.

You can also make arrangements with other local businesses to hand out your materials (flyers, business cards, brochures, and bookmarks, to name a few) in exchange for advertising for them. If you have materials available, be sure to stay alert in regards to community events that may attract your target market. If your business is primarily online, your canvassing area will consist of websites and forums your target customers frequent, as well as individual e-mails. Be sure to do your research and have a list of these places, along with the methods you can use to attract interest there (banner ads, forum memberships, guest blogging, articles, newsletters, and the like).

When planning your materials, make sure you spend some time getting them as attractive and interesting as possible. Comb your wording for spelling and grammatical errors -- not only can these make for a bad first impression to customers, but they can also end up with some unintended consequences. As an extreme example, imagine what would happen if the Motel Six chain missed a typo, and launched an advertising campaign for Motel Sex!

Your mistakes may not be as outrageous, but if you make a mistake in your advertising materials, your customers will be more likely to remember you for your mistakes than the quality of your products or services.

Also, make sure your material is exciting and compelling. Remember your USP? Take the aspect of your business that sets it apart from your competitors and emphasize it in your marketing copy.

If you can come up with a catchy phrase or slogan, a recognizable

icon, or a fun play on words that describes your business, this short and sweet message can go a long way on your materials.

Preparation: Once you've decided on your materials, you have to create them. If you are sending out a small batch of flyers, business cards, or brochures, you may be able to make them yourself with a high-quality printer. A commercial printer is usually more economical for larger quantities. Places like Staples and Kinko's have become more affordable than ever, and there are several competitive online companies like VistaPrint.com to choose from as well.

You will need to supply the printer with a file to print from. With the proliferation of desktop publishing software, you will likely be able to design the materials yourself. However, be sure to invest a lot of time and make it a professional presentation. If you don't feel confident in creating great-looking and sounding promotional material, you may want to consider hiring a freelance designer or copywriter -- you'll pay a one-time price for material you can use over and over.

Distribution: This refers to actually getting the material to your customers. You can distribute flyers yourself, or enlist volunteers to help. Volunteers, partners, or anyone who's willing to spend some time helping you promote may be willing to stand in high-traffic areas like malls or transportation terminals and hand out your material.

You may be mailing out your materials, in which case your distribution involves a trip to the post office. If you're partnering with another local business, you'll simply have to drop off a stack of materials with them.

If you plan an online canvassing campaign, it's a good idea to try and coordinate the various venues and have them hit within the same time frame. Multiple banners, ads, articles, forum posts, blog entries, and e-mails that reach your target audience more than once will help to reinforce your business in their minds, and help them remember you the next time they need your product or service.

Summary

Canvassing is any marketing method that reaches multiple consumers on an individual basis.

There are many forms of canvassing, including flyer and brochure distribution, sampling, telephone or door-to-door marketing, and online campaigns

Canvassing is most effective when you have researched your target market demographic and can access a number of them in the same area.

Other businesses make excellent canvassing partners, since you can reach all of their customers without much effort.

Canvassing relies on a strong message and well-written material to achieve results Distribution, the final step of canvassing, can take place in person, online, or through a third party.

The Sign Says

Signs are everywhere. A good sign can be a great tool for your business, and in true Creative marketing style, it doesn't have to cost much.

What is it?

A sign is any at-a-glance advertisement for your business. They range in size from matchbook covers to billboards, and can be found in a wide variety of locations. Signs are familiar to just about everyone, because there are so many of them. Unfortunately, this means people often overlook them.

How do you do it?

If you want to use signs as part of your Creative marketing campaign, there are two important factors you need to consider: design and placement.

What it should look like

Creating an effective sign means making it stand out from its surroundings, and giving it some individual and memorable characteristics. At the same time, you have to strike a balance between information and clutter.

You may want to consider hiring a professional designer. As with printed advertising materials, the one-time investment often proves worthwhile, since you can use the design over and over again.

However, if you feel confident that you can create your own signs, here are some tips for effective design:

Make sure it's legible from the distance most people will view it. At the least, you will include your website and/or phone number, but if no one can read your sign, they won't contact you for more information.

Speaking of information, don't include too much. The object of a sign is to get people interested in learning more about your business, so don't attempt to close a sale with just your sign.

Apply the KISS principle: Keep It Short & Simple. Elaborate designs and excessive wording will distract rather than attract attention. Ideally, your sign should contain 3 to 10 words in addition to your contact information.

Include a "grabber" element -- either a strong word or phrase in large text, or an intriguing image or company logo.

Pay attention to color scheme, and make sure they are contrasting enough to stand out so everything is easily legible. Some excellent color combinations include black on white, black on yellow, white on black, yellow on black, and blue on white.

What is not there is just as important as what is. You should incorporate approximately 30 to 40 percent of "white space" (not necessarily white, but space with no words or images on it) in the overall design of your sign.

Where to put it

After you design your sign, you'll need to figure out where to put it. Of course, there are the traditional places -- billboards, storefronts, bulletin boards, and the like. You can also get creative and find other places or venues for your signs.

Restroom signs are becoming more popular. Some businesses will allow you to advertise in their bathrooms, and one creative company has actually placed advertisements inside men's urinals with some success.

Roadside placement: Got a house on a road with decent foot or vehicle traffic? How about friends in prime locations? Try placing a sign in your front yard, and recruiting friends to do the same.

Check with community event coordinators -- you may be able to place signs at bake sales, fundraisers, and other local happenings.

Consider swapping signage space with other businesses in your area for greater exposure.

Summary

Though signs are associated with traditional advertising, they can be part of a successful Creative marketing campaign.

A sign is any at-a-glance advertisement for your business.

Design and placement are the two key elements for successful signs.

Creative sign placement can boost your signs' effectiveness.

Vehicle and Body Advertising.

This space for rent: Attractive signs for your business are great, but they are stationary - the only people who see them are those who walk or drive by them. In many ways, mobile signs can attract more attention.

What better way to get your signs in motion than to put them on a moving vehicle... or a moving person?

What is it?

Vehicle advertising: The most obvious examples are the small signs you may have seen on city buses. Transportation companies often rent space on their fleet vehicles to advertisers as an additional source of income. This means anywhere the bus goes, your advertising will be seen by the people in the area, both foot traffic and vehicle traffic.

Other forms of vehicle advertising include:

Interior bus signs.

Taxi and limo billboards Bumper stickers.

Vehicle wraps Self-service.

Body advertising: How about a walking, talking advertisement for your business? You can find people who are willing, for a small fee, to wear temporary tattoos advertising your product or service. These tattoos often make a great conversation piece, and can make a lot of people aware of your business.

How do you do it?

Vehicle advertising: For bus, taxi, and limo advertising, contact your local transportation companies and ask about their ad rates for fleet vehicles. You will probably need to supply your own designs for the ads, but the rates are often fairly inexpensive for the amount of exposure you'll receive. Be sure to spend a lot of time coming up with a catchy advertisement!

You can have custom bumper stickers printed for your business. It's a good idea to feature your (easy to remember) website prominently on a custom bumper sticker. Give them away to family, friends, customers, and at community events. Consider supplying free bumper stickers to other local businesses, to give away to their customers.

Vehicle wraps are partial or full vehicle advertisements that generate some interesting reactions. You pay people -- usually those who drive back and forth to work every day -- to have their personal vehicles "wrapped" with advertisements for your business.

You can also wrap your own personal vehicle, or get body or window detailing done with your business information. No matter where you drive, you will constantly be advertising your product or service!

Body advertising: Your first step here is to design a compelling temporary tattoo that people can identify quickly with your business. Again, it is a good idea to prominently feature your URL in the design, to allow prospective customers to find more information quickly.

When choosing people to wear your temporary tattoos:

Decide how much you're willing to pay each person you recruit. You may want to base this on the number of days the tattoo should remain visible and in good condition.

Specify where the tattoo should be worn. The back of the hand is a good, prominent place, though some advertisers have requested that people place them on their foreheads.

Instruct the recruits as to what information you'd like them to give when people ask about their tattoos. You may want to consider providing them with business cards, brochures, bookmarks, or other promotional items to hand out to those who show interest.

Ask them to keep track of how many people they talk to concerning the tattoos, so you can use the information in your marketing calculations.

Summary

Vehicle and body advertising serve as mobile signs for your business.

There are many different forms of vehicle advertising, some more expensive than others.

Body advertising is enlisting other people to place advertisements for your business on a visible part of their bodies.

Vehicle and body advertisements must be eye-catching and compelling in order to attract interest.

You will need an easy-to-remember URL to incorporate prominently in your vehicle or body advertising design.

Don't forget to enlist yourself, your personal vehicle, and your own body as advertising tools for your business!

Promotional Items

Everyone loves getting free stuff. Promotional items combine this basic element of human psychology with marketing flair for an effective and memorable component of a Creative advertising campaign.

What is it?

A "promotional item" can be any of hundreds of different things. Basically, it's any physical item that bears a printed mention of your business. Your promotional items can be traditional or unique.

You can give them away free, award them to customers for buying certain things or participating in special offers, and even sell them (if they are high quality and in demand) as an additional source of income.

Following is a list of a few traditional and not-so-traditional promotional items that can be customized for your business:

Brochures and sales catalogues Bookmarks.

Printed newsletters Glossy flyers.

Business cards Magnets.

Bumper stickers Key chains.

Coffee mugs Shot glasses Water goblets Tee shirts

Sweatshirts.

Baseball caps Sweatbands Bandannas.

Stress balls.

Stuffed animals Coasters.

Posters.

Matchbooks Lanyards.

Napkins.

Toothpick holders Pens/pencils.

Calendars Tote bags.

Travel clocks Travel mirrors Combs/brushes Box cutters

Towels/washcloths.

How do you do it?

Effective promotional products are intriguing, fitting, and carry just enough information without overburdening your customers. Here are some tips on creating effective promotional items:

Design with signs in mind. Keep the information on promotional products simple and to the point -- include your business name, slogan, and contact information (phone number and/or website). After all, if the item is slathered with text, no one is going to want to actually use it.

Choose items that reflect your business. If you run a catering company, custom napkins and other kitchen items are good choices; whereas combs, brushes, and towels might not be such a good fit. However, just about any promotional item can be adapted to any business with a little creativity.

Make your items fun and attractive. Bookmarks are great, but how many people do you know that actually use them? Unless your main product is a printed book, if you have a bunch of bookmarks made they will probably end up in the trash. Consider what your customers like to do, and base your promotional item decision on your best guess at what will interest them. Custom puzzles, anyone?

Shop around for the best deals. Unless you're creating your promotional items yourself (and it is certainly possible, though time-consuming), you will likely look for a custom printer or manufacturer to emblazon your message on hundreds of items. There are dozens of great places online, including Café Press (www.cafepress.com), which lets you create and purchase your own items at cost, with bulk discounts for larger orders. You might also want to purchase bulk novelty items from a company like the Oriental Trading Company (www.orientaltrading.com) and modify the items yourself.

Distribute your items freely and often. Always keep several promotional items with you, and hand them out constantly. You never know when you'll meet someone who will later become your customer -- and you will at the very least make a bunch of folks happy by giving them free stuff! Don't forget the power of giveaways in conjunction with your main business. Offer to give your promotional items to customers with every purchase. Post the freebie notice in your physical location or on your website, as well as message boards and freebie forums for more exposure.

Summary

A promotional item is any physical, tangible item that bears a message or advertisement for your business.

There are hundreds of promotional items to choose from You can make just about anything into a promotional item.

Promotional items should relate to your business in some way.

Effective promotional items bear simple messages and contact information The best promotional items are fun or useful for your customers.

You should always keep a supply of promotional items on hand.

Chapter 4 – Digital Creative Marketing

Whether your business is a traditional store, a work-from-home operation, or a completely online venture, a strong web presence is a must in today's fast-paced marketing world. In the age of instant information, businesses without websites have a decided disadvantage.

One of the most important things to keep in mind when it comes to online marketing is that despite the instantaneous nature of the Internet, there are no overnight success methods. Just like a live marketing campaign, your online Creative marketing efforts will require time and effort in order to succeed.

In this chapter, we'll discuss the ins and outs of online promotion, and learn some Creative marketing techniques you can use to further your business on the Internet, whether or not it's based online.

Establishing yourself

If you want customers, you need to make people aware of your website. You also have to make sure your website is a good place to be. Your basic goals with online marketing are to generate traffic to your website, and to keep visitors there when they arrive (and keep them coming back).

We'll talk about this in reverse order, since you need your website up and running before you start attracting visitors.

Website basics

A website can be a very powerful marketing tool. However, a bad website can have a powerful but opposing effect: driving off not only current visitors, but also everyone they know, when they start telling everyone on the 'net how terrible your website looks, or how difficult it is to navigate.

Keep in mind that there are millions of websites out there, and if yours does not attract a visitor's attention with their first look, they'll simply go to the next page of search results and give their business to someone else.

Does your website pass the first-look test? Here are some rules to keep in mind:

Your URL, or website address (www.YourWebSite.com) should be easy to remember and spell, and contain very few, if any, special characters or alternate spellings. This not only looks more professional when visitors find a link to your website online, but it also makes it much easier to translate real-world advertisements into website visitors. You should include your URL on all of your physical marketing material.

Your home page should be visually pleasing, easy to read, and not cluttered with text. Make sure all of your important information is contained in the top portion of your home page (the area visible on a screen when a visitor first arrives at the site) -- but do not try to cram everything on the home page. Include links to essential pages rather than lengthy descriptions of everything.

Flash animation is great, but a huge flash presentation on your home page not only slows down your load time (to the point where visitors will not bother waiting for the page to display), but also turns off many casual Internet users. If you must use Flash animation, keep it to a minimum and don't use it to convey essential information.

If you have a newsletter, include an e-mail link or a subscription box on every page of your website. The more visible your options are, the greater the chances people will find them.

Your website should be an informative place. A hard-sell website ("This product/service is amazing! Buy it now!") does not appeal to most Web browsers. Be sure to post news and current events concerning your business, and consider providing informative articles that educate visitors on topics pertaining to your products or services.

Update often. Keeping your content fresh not only makes search engines happy, it also provides visitors with a reason to keep coming back!

Make your content keyword-rich without being blatant. Brainstorm a list of search terms Internet users might type into a search engine when looking for a website like yours, and use each of those terms a few times. Do not clump together lists of keywords; instead, sprinkle them throughout your content. The practice of keyword stuffing can get your website banned from search engines.

Be user-friendly! Test your website using several different screen resolutions to make sure the text and images are not too crowded or spread out. Check your links and navigation controls frequently -- few things are more frustrating to an Internet user than dead or outdated links. Make sure every page includes a link to your home page and a link to your sales or "landing" page, at the very least.

Internet marketing basics

Just about all "traditional" forms of Internet marketing can be classified as Creative marketing. This is because Internet advertising is generally inexpensive or free, involves an investment of your time and effort, and must be presented in a unique manner if you want to stand out from the millions of other websites competing for attention.

It is a good idea to incorporate basic Internet marketing into your Creative campaign. If you have never promoted a website before, you may not be familiar with the basic concepts of spreading the e-word.

Here are a few ideas to get you started (remember, all these tactics should be implemented after your website is optimized, fine-tuned, double-checked and ready for business).

The more search engines your website is listed on, the greater the chance customers will stumble across it.

The "big" search engines such as Google and Yahoo! do not allow manual submissions, but your website will automatically be picked up within a few weeks by their web trawlers. However, smaller search engines like AltaVista, Dogpile, and ExactSeek may not automatically include your site. There are many free search engine submission programs online that will submit your website to multiple engines for inclusion. Be sure to have a list of keywords and a brief (two to three sentences) description of your website available while you're submitting.

If you have a newsletter, you can list your website in multiple newsletter or e-zine directories in the same way you submit to search engine. Having a free, regular newsletter or e-zine that contains interesting and informative material is a great way to build customer loyalty and attract new business online. Your subscribers will be more likely to purchase your products or services, since they will see your business multiple times.

Banner ad exchange programs are another possibility for Internet exposure. When you design your banner ad, keep in mind the rules for creating an effective sign and apply them to the banner. If you don't have any computer experience, there are several programs that will allow you to generate a banner ad using their template for free. Then, seek similar or complementary websites to your business and offer to host their banner in exchange for hosting theirs on your website.

Pay-per-click (PPC) advertising is effective in many cases, and though it does require a monetary investment, the amount is small (usually 2 to 5 cents per visitor). One example of a good pay-per-click program is Google AdWords (http://adwords.google.com) -- the program does not require minimum monthly spending, and the average bidding rate for lesser search terms is 2 to 3 cents. Google also includes a keyword generator to help you write more effective ads. More information is available through the preceding link.

Going Viral

Viral marketing is one of the most powerful forms of Internet advertising available. It takes basic online marketing a step further: basically, you get the ball rolling, and hundreds of other Internet users pick it up and run with it.

What is it?

Viral marketing is more or less the Internet term for word-of-mouth. The term "viral marketing" refers to any advertising method that encourages people who receive a message to pass it on to others.

One classic example of a viral marketing strategy was demonstrated by Microsoft Networks Hotmail program. Hotmail was one of the first free web-based e-mail providers. In order to let people know about the program, Microsoft included a tag or signature at the bottom of every outgoing e-mail their customers sent, reading: "Get your private, free e-mail at http://www.hotmail.com", that was linked to Hotmail's main page. People receiving messages from users with Hotmail accounts set up their own, and then e-mailed more people with the same tag on every message. The number of Hotmail users ballooned in no time.

In essence, Microsoft invented the e-mail signature, another powerful marketing tool now used by millions online.

Keep in mind that viral marketing does not simply spread your message from person to person. Effective viral marketing spreads from person to people, making your advertising program an exponential success.

How do you do it?

The best way to engage in viral marketing online is to make it easy for your customers to spread your message. There are quite a few ways to do this:

Newsletters or e-zines: Since most newsletters and e-zines are delivered via e-mail, it's easy for your customers to hit forward and pass them on to several friends.

However, this will only happen if you include good, quality information in your electronic publication. Rather than simply advertising your products or services, consider writing articles, hosting guest columns, and generally providing your customers with something fun.

Article syndication: Once you have written articles for your newsletter or e-zine, share the knowledge by uploading them to article syndication websites.

These are "article banks" used by web masters looking for fresh content for their own websites.

Essentially, you are giving anyone permission to reprint your article, with the caveat that your authorship and a link to your website is included. Article syndication creates inbound links that boost your website's search engine rank, and make it more likely customers will find you.

Refer-a-friend programs: Got something valuable to give your customers, such as bonus products or promotional items? Consider using a refer-a-friend program: in exchange for providing you with a number of e-mail addresses to which you can send a one-time announcement about your business, you can give your customers something they'll enjoy, and make them eager to tell their friends about your website.

Link-swapping and banner placement: As mentioned in the previous section, the more links there are on the Internet leading to your website, the greater your exposure will be. Offer to host other websites' links and banner ads on your site in exchange for a reciprocal link from theirs.

Also, keep in mind that inbound links (links that point to your website, and are not linked back from your website) carry more weight with search engines than outbound or reciprocal links. Try to post as many inbound links as you can.

Giveaways, contests, and freebies: Once again, everyone loves to get something for nothing. Sponsoring contests and giveaways will naturally generate the urge for your customers to tell others about your website, so everyone they know can get the free deal or enter the contest. Don't hesitate to give away the occasional product or service in exchange for the marketing value it can bring your business!

Online communities and forums: Joining forums and communities dedicated to topics that will interest your customers is a great way to get your name out there.
Remember, online etiquette dictates that you do not simply join a forum and immediately post advertisements. Spend some time getting to know other forum members, and they will be happy to tell others in the community about you and your business.

As with other forms of advertising, your message has to be compelling and interesting, or no one will want to pass it on. Make sure to spend as much time developing your advertising message as you do spreading it around. Don't forget to include your USP, any promotions or freebies you may be running, and your website and contact information.

Summary

Viral marketing is the Internet form of word-of-mouth.

The keys to viral marketing are to create a compelling message and make it easy for people to pass it on.

Viral marketing represents an exponential increase in online exposure for your business.

There are several different viral marketing methods you can take advantage of for your website.

Viral marketing messages must be interesting, informative, or valuable in order to be successfully spread.

Beating the Blog Drum

Do you blog? Even if you don't, chances are you have already seen several blogs online, though you might not be aware of this relatively new website format.

Blogs

create a sense of community and provide an outlet for many different types of information, both business and personal.

What is it?

Blog, short for web log, is a specialized type of website that acts like an electronic journal. Blog users can type in text, upload pictures and sound, and instantly post it to the site. Blog software formats each entry in the blog style you select, automatically creates entry archives and permanent links to each page, and allows for easy customization.

Most blogs also allow comments from visitors. There are comment screening options you can use to disallow anonymous comments, comments from non-bloggers, or comments altogether. However, the comments feature is one of the most powerful components of a blog, because visitors can enjoy instant interaction with you.

Blogs allow you to speak with your customers on a personal level. Once Internet users get to know the person behind the business, they will be more likely to purchase your products or services. Trust is a valuable commodity online, and blogs help you build up a trust bank.

Best of all, most blogs are free to create and use, so you won't have to spend a penny on your blog.

A few of the most popular blog providers are:

Blogger -- www.blogger.com: Owned by Google. Fully featured free blogs with customizable templates, easy to use.

LiveJournal - www.livejournal.com: Similar to Blogger, offers paid upgrades for additional special features.

WordPress - www.wordpress.com: Another popular free blogger platform with millions of users, easy interfaces and lots of template choices Blogs have become so popular, there are millions of bloggers (people with blogs) online communicating tons of information, opinions, and chats every day. In fact, the blog collective on the Internet has become powerful enough to merit its own term: the blogosphere. The blogosphere as a whole is extremely influential, and often when one blog carries an item of interest, others will pick it up and spread it across the Internet.

How do you do it?

Using a blog for business purposes is a twofold process. First, you have to build a readership for your blog. Then, you can enlist other bloggers to help you get more exposure for yours.

Building a readership

Like your website, you should plan to keep your blog informative and entertaining, and update regularly. Many bloggers post to their blogs daily, and often include links to other websites with news or information they believe may interest their readers. It is a good idea to choose a posting schedule (daily, Monday through Friday, bi-weekly, weekly -- whatever you're comfortable keeping up with) and stick to it.

The single most effective way to gain readers for your blog is to visit other people's blogs and leave thoughtful comments on their posts. Do not simply comment that you have a blog and you want them to visit; this is viewed as spam, or at the very least, rude.

Of course, contacting individual bloggers is a time-consuming process. Another way to attract readers is to list your blog in as many blog directories as you can find. This way, Internet users will be able to find your blog through search engines.

Post a link to your blog on your website, and include one in your e-mail signature. The more people know about your blog, the more likely you will be to get visitors.

Working in the blogosphere

Other bloggers are an excellent marketing resource. Most blogging software includes an easy tool to add links to your sidebar. You can link to several other blogs that may be of interest to your readers -- and in most cases, the bloggers you link to will automatically link back to your blog, since this is considered common courtesy. Some bloggers will list an e-mail address you can contact them through to exchange blog links. Take advantage of these when you find them. You can also participate in guest blogging -- writing an entry for someone else's blog for a day. Since bloggers always need fresh content, many are happy to host other people's articles as long as they pertain to their readers. Find blogs that are similar to yours and request to be a guest blogger. Remember to include a link to your website at the end of your post!

Summary

Blogs are a specialized form of website that act like online journals.

The millions of blogs online are collectively known as the blogosphere Bloggers (people who blog) and blog readers are very influential online.

Most blogs are free to set up, and have easy templates that don't require HTML coding knowledge.

Like your website, your blog should be informative, entertaining, and updated regularly Visit other people's blogs and link to them to get increased traffic for your blog.

Becoming a guest blogger is a great way to get more exposure for your business.

Chapter 5 – Rules and Regulations

Following the rules is an important step in Creative marketing. Some people view Creative marketing tactics as too aggressive, and many a marketer has been threatened with legal action.

However, if you're familiar with what you can and cannot do, you will not have to worry about this. Make sure you protect yourself!

Fairness in Advertising

Honesty is still the best policy. Consumers don't appreciate being lied to, and nothing spreads faster -- both online and in your community -- than news of a dishonest business.

Therefore, it's important that you practice fairness in advertising.

What It Means

Fairness in advertising is really a simple concept: don't claim your product or service does something that it doesn't. For example, a diet pill company claiming their product will "make you lose 50 pounds overnight!" is clearly mistaken -- this is a physical impossibility, unless you amputate your legs. Even with a quantifier like "practically" or "almost" (You'll lose 50 pounds practically overnight!), the statement remains implausible. Every person's idea of "practically" is different.

What would be fair for our fictitious diet pill company to claim? It depends on what the product actually does. In this scenario, the company may be able to state that their diet pill helps you lose weight "faster than the leading brands" or even that you may notice results "practically overnight" (not 50 pounds worth of results, of course!).

Your wording is essential when practicing fairness in advertising. You can get creative, but there is a fine line between creativity and false claims. In most cases, it's best to let your product or service speak for itself.

Customer testimonials are an excellent way to incorporate fairness in advertising. Getting real statements from the people who have used your product or service not only keeps you honest, but also allows consumers to trust you more, because the opinions are coming from someone who has no vested interest in your business.

Don't lie to your customers, and they will thank you with their business.

Spam Isn't Healthy

One of the most pervasive myths in online advertising today is this: the more people you e-mail, the more money you'll make. But if you're using bulk e-mail to get there, you're on the wrong track.

No one likes spam. In the Internet world, the term "spam" refers to any e-mail advertising a product or service that you did not ask to receive (and not the lunchmeat-in-a-can pictured above). There are a lot of marketing "gurus" who insist that sending cold bulk e-mails still gets results -- and that may have been true when the Internet was still in its infancy, but today's online community is more perceptive than ever, and it's almost impossible to slip by the collective spam radar.

If you look, you can find several hundred places that will sell you lists of thousands of e-mail addresses for a few dollars. The temptation to buy these lists is strong... who can resist thousands of potential customers in one shot, without the many hours of research it takes to build a solid opt-in list of your own?

You can! Here's why you should:

Spamming alienates potential customers. When people receive spam, often their first reaction is to delete it unread, and most will block all further communication from that particular e-mail address: yours.

Many Internet users hate spam so much, they will take action to shut you down. This can range from reporting you to your ISP (Internet service provider), to flaming (sending hate mail) or "mail bombs" (sending hundreds or thousands of files with very large attachments designed to crash your server).

Your business can be blacklisted. There is an actual Internet advertiser's blacklist that warns consumers about spammers, and you don't want to be connected with that list.

Spamming just plain doesn't work! There are so many dangerous scams online today that most Internet users are reluctant to even open any unsolicited messages. Even if you write the most brilliant and enticing advertising message in the world, if you send it through bulk e-mail, no one will ever read it.

In short: don't spam. Do the work and create your own list of people who actually want to hear what you have to say. Your business will benefit enormously, and you won't be branded as a charlatan.

Weird Laws and Ordinances

As a Creative marketer, it's important for you to obey the law. If a customer feels you are trying to con them, skirt legal issues, or harass them into buying your product or service, you could end up with a lot more trouble than a lost sale.

You can familiarize yourself with basic marketing dos and don'ts through the Federal Trade Commission (FTC), the government organization that regulates and protects

consumers in the United States. Browse their website at www.ftc.gov for more information on advertising guidance, antitrust laws, and FTC procedures regarding consumer complaints.

You should also check with your local Chamber of Commerce, and request information on advertising laws that affect your business. Find the nearest Chamber to you here: http://www.uschamber.com/chambers/directory/default

Does your city or state have strange laws that forbid a certain Creative marketing method? The website Dumb Laws (www.dumblaws.com) provides a collection of weird, outrageous and outlandish laws that are still on the books. Here is a sampling of some laws that might hinder your marketing efforts:

In Alabama, it is illegal to impersonate a person of the clergy -- so don't dress up as a priest to promote your business.

You can be fined $25 for flirting in New York. Beware of approaching strangers!

Speaking of truth in advertising, a jail term of up to one year awaits you in Louisiana for making a false promise.

Watch out, mobile billboard advertisers in Ohio: the Ohio driver's education manual states that you must honk the horn when you pass another vehicle.

In Texas, it is illegal to sell one's eye. Keep your body parts close at hand.

Florida forbids "unnatural acts" with another person... so forget playing Twister on the sidewalk. Also, it's illegal to skateboard without a license.

Unless you own at least two cows, you may not wear cowboy boots in California.

Seasonal business owners should note that in Maine, you will be fined for displaying Christmas decorations after January 14.

Your profits will come in handy in Illinois, where you can be arrested for vagrancy if you don't have at least one dollar on your person.

What strange laws does your state have? Perhaps one of them will give you an idea for your Creative marketing campaign!

Chapter 6 – Welcome to the Jungle

Are you ready to become a Creative?

Without a doubt, Creative marketing is an extremely effective strategy for any small business. Since you typically will not have a huge advertising budget, it makes more sense to invest effort and time, and reap the rewards of your careful planning and creativity.

Some points to remember:

You will get out of your Creative marketing campaign what you put into it. If you do not invest the effort, you will not reap the rewards.

A successful Creative marketing campaign is ongoing, and consists of more than one strategy or tactic.

Be patient: Creative success will not come to you overnight, but it will come!

Think outside the box (in fact, try to come up with your own term for thinking outside the box as an exercise in creativity). The unique aspects of your business will generate better profits when you leverage them.

Do not view other businesses as your competition. Instead, view them as potential partners and cultivate mutually beneficial relationships.

Never pass up an opportunity to market (but keep it casual where it's appropriate to refrain from being pushy).

Be prepared to watch your business leap forward!

Creative marketing is not just a strategy... it's a state of mind. When you learn to think like a Creative, you will greatly improve your business marketing skills -- not to mention your profits.

Positive reviews from awesome customers like you help others to feel confident about choosing this book. Thanks very much !

"Santiago Johnson Smith"

DISCLAIMER AND TERMS OF USE AGREEMENT:

The author and publisher of this course and the accompanying materials have used their best efforts in preparing this course. The author and publisher make no representation or warranties with respect to the accuracy, applicability, fitness, or completeness of the contents of this course. The information contained in this course is strictly for educational purposes. Therefore, if you wish to apply ideas contained in this course, you are taking full responsibility for your actions.

Every effort has been made to accurately represent this product and it's potential. Even though this industry is one of the few where one can write their own check in terms of earnings, there is no guarantee that you will earn any money using the techniques and ideas in these materials. Examples in these materials are not to be interpreted as a promise or guarantee of earnings.

Continue to the next page...